BETWEEN EARTH AND SKY

Neil Philip was born in York in 1955, and has degrees from the universities of Oxford and London. Since 1979 he has made his living as a freelance critic and journalist, writing documentary film scripts as well as contributing essays and reviews to a wide range of journals. He is reviews editor of *Folklore* and is the author of *A Fine Anger: A Critical Introduction to the Work of Alan Garner* (1981). His short play for voices about the poet John Clare, *Her Who Is Never Forgotten*, was performed at the Tower Theatre Club, Islington, in May 1982. A book of his essays, *Bright Trains of Images*, is in preparation. He is married and lives in Oxford.

BETWEEN EARTH AND SKY

POETRY AND PROSE OF ENGLISH RURAL LIFE AND WORK
BETWEEN THE ENCLOSURES AND THE GREAT WAR

Compiled by Neil Philip

PENGUIN BOOKS

Penguin Books Ltd, Harmondsworth, Middlesex, England
Penguin Books, 40 West 23rd Street, New York, New York 10010, U.S.A.
Penguin Books Australia Ltd, Ringwood, Victoria, Australia
Penguin Books Canada Ltd, 2801 John Street, Markham, Ontario, Canada L3R 1B4
Penguin Books (N.Z.) Ltd, 182–190 Wairau Road, Auckland 10, New Zealand

This compilation was published in 1984
Compilation and Introduction copyright © Neil Philip, 1984
All rights reserved

The Acknowledgements on pages 263–5 constitute an extension
of this copyright page

Reproduced, printed and bound in Great Britain by
Hazell Watson & Viney Limited,
Member of the BPCC Group,
Aylesbury, Bucks
Filmset in Linotron Baskerville by
Rowland Phototypesetting Ltd,
Bury St Edmunds, Suffolk

Title page illustration by Sally Seymour

TO MY PARENTS

'Well, 'tis only for life. If 'twas for
longer than that I don't know if we should
hardly be able to bear it.'

Old woman, quoted in George Bourne,
Change in the Village

'Luck nearly always follows after
misfortune. If this were not so,
people would soon die out.'

Qúpaq, Netsilik Eskimo, quoted in
Knud Rasmussen, *The Netsilik Eskimos*

CONTENTS

INTRODUCTION

I T is easy to be nostalgic for a past you did not have to live through. The life of the English farmworker in the nineteenth century was not easy. It was ruled by poverty and hard work. Nevertheless it was a life lived in community with others, a life lived close to the land, a life lived in tradition. This book chronicles the last period of that tradition, from the large-scale enclosure of common land in the late eighteenth and early nineteenth centuries to the outbreak of the First World War in 1914.

Enclosure, though it greatly increased agricultural productivity, dispossessed the labourer of the land. 'This scythe of desolation', the poet Robert Bloomfield called it. Yet still the old life lingered on, until the war and the internal combustion engine made the scythe a symbol of harmless rusticity and gave us new images of desolation. Many of the countrymen who fought in the Great War had scarcely left their villages before. Many of them never returned. Those who did entered the modern world.

Now, when we barely notice the turn of the seasons, when we eat out of packets and live in a fragmented society, it is easy to look at the life which has gone with sentimental eyes. Indeed, throughout history people have looked back to the recent rural past as a golden age. John Clare, a labourer himself and a labourer's son, saw the Helpston of his childhood, before its enclosure, as the garden of Eden. But Clare, though he wrote of the changes he saw with a fierce sense of loss, did not romanticize. He knew well that traditional rural communities were not simply supportive, rooted, dignified, but also suspicious, inflexible, coarse. 'I live here among the ignorant like a lost man,' he wrote.

I have tried to balance in this anthology the happiness and the deprivation. Those who yearn for a more bucolic picture should remember that when John Clare was starving by the roadside in July 1841 (he ate first 'a good many wishes for breakfast but wishes was no hearty meal', then grass 'which seemed to taste something like bread'), passers-by saw nothing unusual. 'Somewhere on the London side [of] the "Plough" public-house a man passed me on horseback in a slop-frock & said "here's another of the broken-down haymakers" & threw me a penny to get a half pint of beer.' As William Dawson exclaimed to the Rector of Upwell in East Anglia twenty-five years earlier, 'Here I am, between Earth and Sky – so help me God. I would sooner loose my life than go home as I am. Bread I want and Bread I will have.'

George Sturt (George Bourne), writing of the traditional life described in this book, had this to say, in a journal entry for 28 May 1906:

Though there was much that was good, it was bought too dear. I think especially of the peasantry. The women grew prematurely old: the children early lost their charm: the loveliness of the girls was gone almost before they had grown up. One may judge it, by those amongst whom the old mode of living still survives. The waste of beauty is heart-rending.

We should not idealize the workfolk in these pages, or their way of life. But if we cannot wholeheartedly envy them, we can celebrate them. We certainly cannot look down on them, seeing how much they made of their little, and how little we make of our much.

This book makes no claim to completeness. It is not an agricultural or social history of the times, though it covers a period of great and complex change; the many questions it leaves aside may be tracked down through the volumes listed as 'Further Reading'.

The sources are various. Although I am aware of the mass of material I have not drawn on, only one likely category was deliberately excluded from consideration: dialect verse. I feel that, in isolation, dialect poems, even those of William Barnes, tend to render quaint a picture I wanted to keep in sharp, not soft, focus. The severest artificial restriction was the relative lack of direct evidence from women. Flora Thompson's is still a lonely voice, finding its echo not in other accounts but in Elizabeth Ashby's 'I could have a lot to say but silence becomes me best.'

What I have tried to convey, by selection and juxtaposition, is something of the inwardness of a life which has usually been described, when it has been noticed at all, from outside. Even Richard Jefferies, an acute and sensitive observer of English country life, condescended to the labouring class he described so well. To Jefferies, as to most of his contemporaries, all farm labourers were 'Hodge': a communal being without culture or wit. You will not find Hodge in these pages, but a selection of individuals, like Cobbett, 'born in a cottage, and bred to the plough'.

My thanks are due to the librarians and staffs of the British Library, the Bodleian Library, the University of London Library and Goldsmith's Library, the Folklore Society, the English Folk Dance and Song Society and the Museum of English Rural Life at Reading University. I also gratefully acknowledge the help and suggestions of Emma Bradford, Sylvia Bradford, Victor E. Neuburg and John Philip, and the interest and encouragement of Donald McFarlan, Martin West, Sophie Burn, Kate Hamilton and David Grogan at Penguin.

NEIL PHILIP *Oxford, 24 September 1982*

I

A Charm

TAKE of English earth as much
  As either hand may rightly clutch.
In the taking of it breathe
Prayer for all who lie beneath –
Not the great nor well-bespoke,
But the mere uncounted folk
Of whose life and death is none
Report or lamentation.
    Lay that earth upon thy heart,
    And thy sickness shall depart!

It shall sweeten and make whole
Fevered breath and festered soul;
It shall mightily restrain
Over-busy hand and brain;
It shall ease thy mortal strife
'Gainst the immortal woe of life,
Till thyself restored shall prove
By what grace the Heavens do move.

Take of English flowers these –
Spring's full-facéd primroses,
Summer's wild wide-hearted rose,
Autumn's wall-flower of the close,
And, thy darkness to illume,
Winter's bee-thronged ivy-bloom.

Seek and serve them where they bide
From Candlemas to Christmas-tide,
   For these simples used aright
   Shall restore a failing sight.

These shall cleanse and purify
Webbed and inward-turning eye;
These shall show thee treasure hid,
Thy familiar fields amid,
At thy threshold, on thy hearth,
Or about thy daily path;
And reveal (which is thy need)
Every man a King indeed!

RUDYARD KIPLING

2

Cock-Crow

Out of the wood of thoughts that grows by night
  To be cut down by the sharp axe of light, –
Out of the night, two cocks together crow,
Cleaving the darkness with a silver blow:
And bright before my eyes twin trumpeters stand,
Heralds of splendour, one at either hand,
Each facing each as in a coat of arms:
The milkers lace their boots up at the farms.

EDWARD THOMAS

T HE ordinary adult farm labourer commonly rises at from four to five o'clock; if he is a milker, and has to walk some little distance to his work, even as early as half-past three. Four was the general rule, but of late years the hour has grown later. He milks till five or half-past, carries the yokes to the dairy, and draws water for the dairymaid, or perhaps chops up some wood for her fire to scald the milk. At six he goes to breakfast, which consists of a hunch of bread and cheese as a rule, with now and then a piece of bacon, and as a milker he receives his quart of beer. At breakfast there is no hurry for half-an-hour or so; but some time before seven he is on at the ordinary work of the day. If a milker and very early riser, he is not usually put at the heavy jobs, but allowances are made for the work he has already done. The other men on the farm arrive at six. At eleven, or half-past, comes luncheon, which lasts a full hour, often an hour and a quarter. About three o'clock the task of milking again com-mences; the buckets are got out with a good deal of rattling and noise, the yokes fitted to the shoulders, and away he goes for an hour or hour and a half of milking. That done, he has to clean up the court and help the dairymaid put the heavier articles in place; then another quart of beer, and away home. The time of leaving off work varies from half-past five to half-past six. At ordinary seasons the other men leave at six, but in haymaking or harvest time they are expected to remain till the job in hand that day is finished, often till eight or half-past.

RICHARD JEFFERIES

THE thresher first thro darkness deep
  Awakes the mornings winter sleep
Scaring the owlet from her prey
Long before she dreams of day
That blinks above head on the snow
Watching the mice that squeaks below
And foddering boys sojourn again
By ryhme hung hedge and frozen plain
Shuffling thro the sinking snows
Blowing his fingers as he goes
To where the stock in bellowings hoarse
Call for their meals in dreary close
And print full many a hungry track
Round circling hedge that guards the stack
Wi higgling tug he cuts the hay
And bares the forkfull loads away
And morn and evening daily throws
The little heaps upon the snows
The shepherd too in great coat wrapt
And straw bands round his stockings lapt
Wi plodding dog that sheltering steals
To shun the wind behind his heels
Takes rough and smooth the winter weather
And paces thro the snow together
While in the fields the lonly plough
Enjoys its frozen sabbath now

JOHN CLARE

On Giles, and such as Giles, the labour falls,
  To strew the frequent load where hunger calls.
On driving gales sharp hail indignant flies,
And sleet, more irksome still, assails his eyes;
Snow clogs his feet; or if no snow is seen,
The field with all its juicy store to screen,
Deep goes the frost, till every root is found
A rolling mass of ice upon the ground.
No tender ewe can break her nightly fast,
Nor heifer strong begin the cold repast,
Till Giles with pond'rous beetle foremost go,
And scatt'ring splinters fly at every blow;
When pressing round him, eager for the prize,
From their mixt breath warm exhalations rise.

ROBERT BLOOMFIELD

6

When this old hat was new

I am a poor old man, come listen to my song.
  Provisions now are twice as dear as when that I was young;
When this old hat was new and stood above my brow,
Oh! what a happy youth was I when this old hat was new.

But four score year ago, the truth I do declare,
When men they took each other's word, they thought it very
    fair,
No oaths they did require, men's words they were so true,
'Twas thus all in my youthful days when this old hat was new.

And when the harvest came and we went off to shear,
How often we were merry made with brandy, ale and beer;
When corn it was brought home and put upon the mow,
The workers' paunches were well fill'd when this old hat was
    new.

At the board's head stood the farmer, the table for to grace,
And greeted all as they came in, each took his proper place;
His wife stood at the table to give each man his due,
And Oh! what plenty did abound when this old hat was new.

But how the times are chang'd, the poor are quite done o'er,
They give to them their wages like beggars at the door;
In the house we must not go, although we are but few,
It was not so when Bess did reign and this old hat was new.

The commons are taken in and cottages pull'd down,
Moll has got no wool to spin her linsey-wolsey gown;
'Tis cold and clothing's thin and blankets are but few,
But we were cloth'd both back and side when this old hat was
    new.

When Romans rul'd this land, the commons they did give
Unto the poor in charity to help them for to live;
The poor are quite done o'er, we know it to be true,
It was not so when Bess did reign and this old hat was new.

                                                    TRADITIONAL

Sally could just remember the rise when it still stood in a wide expanse of open heath, with juniper bushes and furze thickets and close, springy, rabbit-bitten turf. There were only six houses then and they stood in a ring round an open green, all with large gardens and fruit trees and faggot piles. Laura could pick out most of the houses, still in a ring, but lost to sight of each other among the newer, meaner dwellings that had sprung up around and between them. Some of the houses had been built on and made into two, others had lost their lean-tos and outbuildings. Only Sally's remained the same, and Sally was eighty. Laura in her lifetime was to see a ploughed field where Sally's stood; but had she been told that she would not have believed it.

Country people had not been so poor when Sally was a girl, or their prospects so hopeless. Sally's father had kept a cow, geese, poultry, pigs, and a donkey-cart to carry his produce to the market town. He could do this because he had commoners' rights and could turn his animals out to graze, and cut furze for firing and even turf to make a lawn for one of his customers. Her mother made butter, for themselves and to sell, baked their own bread, and made candles for lighting. Not much of a light, Sally said, but it cost next to nothing, and, of course, they went to bed early.

Sometimes her father would do a day's work for wages, thatching a rick, cutting and laying a hedge, or helping with the shearing or the harvest. This provided them with ready money for boots and clothes; for food they relied almost entirely on home produce. Tea was a luxury seldom indulged in, for it cost five shillings a pound. But country people then had not acquired the taste for tea; they preferred home-brewed.

Everybody worked; the father and mother from daybreak to dark. Sally's job was to mind the cow and drive the geese to the best grass patches. It was strange to picture Sally, a little girl, running with her switch after the great hissing birds on the common, especially as both common and geese had vanished as completely as though they had never been.

FLORA THOMPSON

8

WHERE is the Common, once with blessings rich –
    The poor man's Common? – like the poor man's flitch
And well-fed ham, which erst his means allow'd,
'Tis gone to bloat the idle and the proud!

EBENEZER ELLIOTT

9
The Mores

FAR spread the moorey ground a level scene
    Bespread with rush and one eternal green
That never felt the rage of blundering plough
Though centurys wreathed springs blossoms on its brow
Still meeting plains that stretched them far away
In uncheckt shadows of green brown and grey
Unbounded freedom ruled the wandering scene
Nor fence of ownership crept in between
To hide the prospect of the following eye
Its only bondage was the circling sky

One mighty flat undwarfed by bush and tree
Spread its faint shadow of immensity
And lost itself which seemed to eke its bounds
In the blue mist the orisons edge surrounds

Now this sweet vision of my boyish hours
Free as spring clouds and wild as summer flowers
Is faded all – a hope that blossomed free
And hath been once no more shall ever be
Inclosure came and trampled on the grave
Of labours rights and left the poor a slave
And memorys pride ere want to wealth did bow
Is both the shadow and the substance now
The sheep and cows were free to range as then
Where change might prompt nor felt the bonds of men
Cows went and came with evening morn and night
To the wild pasture as their common right
And sheep unfolded with the rising sun
Heard the swains shout and felt their freedom won
Tracked the red fallow field and heath and plain
Then met the brook and drank and roamed again
The brook that dribbled on as clear as glass
Beneath the roots they hid among the grass
While the glad shepherd traced their tracks along
Free as the lark and happy as her song
But now alls fled and flats of many a dye
That seemed to lengthen with the following eye
Moors loosing from the sight far smooth and blea
Where swopt the plover in its pleasure free
Are vanished now with commons wild and gay
As poets visions of lifes early day
Mulberry bushes where the boy would run
To fill his hands with fruit are grubbed and done

And hedgrow briars – flower lovers overjoyed
Came and got flower pots – these are all destroyed
And sky bound mores in mangled garbs are left
Like mighty giants of their limbs bereft
Fence now meets fence in owners little bounds
Of field and meadow large as garden grounds
In little parcels little minds to please
With men and flocks imprisoned ill at ease
Each little path that led its pleasant way
As sweet as morning leading night astray
Where little flowers bloomed round a varied host
That travel felt delighted to be lost
Nor grudged the steps that he had taen as vain
When right roads traced his journeys and again
Nay on a broken tree hed sit awhile
To see the mores and fields and meadows smile
Sometimes with cowslaps smothered – then all white
With daiseys – then the summers splendid sight
Of corn fields crimson oer the 'headach' bloomd
Like splendid armys for the battle plumed
He gazed upon them with wild fancys eye
As fallen landscapes from an evening sky
These paths are stopt – the rude philistines thrall
Is laid upon them and destroyed them all
Each little tyrant with his little sign
Shows where man claims earth glows no more divine
But paths to freedom and to childhood dear
A board sticks up to notice 'no road here'
And on the tree with ivy overhung
The hated sign by vulgar taste is hung
As tho the very birds should learn to know
When they go there they must no further go
This with the poor scared freedom bade good bye
And much they feel it in the smothered sigh

And birds and trees and flowers without a name
All sighed when lawless laws enclosure came
And dreams of plunder in such rebel schemes
Have found too truly that they were but dreams

JOHN CLARE

10

To the enclosure of the common more than to any other cause may be traced all the changes that have subsequently passed over the village. It was like knocking the keystone out of an arch. The keystone is not the arch; but, once it is gone, all sorts of forces, previously resisted, begin to operate towards ruin, and gradually the whole structure crumbles down. This fairly illustrates what has happened to the village, in consequence of the loss of the common. The direct results have been perhaps the least important in themselves; but indirectly the enclosure mattered, because it left the people helpless against influences which have sapped away their interests, robbed them of security and peace, rendered their knowledge and skill of small value, and seriously affected their personal pride and their character. Observe it well. The enclosure itself, I say, was not actually the cause of all this; but it was the opening, so to speak, through which all this was let in. The other causes which have been at work could hardly have operated as they have done if the village life had not been weakened by the changes directly due to the loss of the common.

They consisted – those changes – in a radical alteration of the domestic economy of the cottagers. Not suddenly, but none the less inevitably, the old thrift – the peasant thrift – which the people understood thoroughly had to be abandoned in favour of a modern thrift – commercial thrift – which they understood but vaguely. That was the essential effect of the enclosure, the central change directly caused by it; and it struck at the very heart of the peasant system.

For note what it involved. By the peasant system, as I have already explained, people derived the necessaries of life from the materials and soil of their own countryside. Now, so long as they had the common, the inhabitants of the valley were in a large degree able to conform to this system, the common being, as it were, a supplement to the cottage gardens, and furnishing means of extending the scope of the little home industries. It encouraged the poorest labourer to practise, for instance, all those time-honoured crafts which Cobbett, in his little book on Cottage Economy, had advocated as the one hope for labourers. The cow-keeping, the bread-making, the fattening of pigs and curing of bacon, were actually carried on here thirty years after Cobbett's time, besides other things not mentioned by him, such as turf-cutting on the heath and wheat-growing in the gardens. But it was the common that made all this possible. It was only by the spacious 'turn-out' which it afforded that the people were enabled to keep cows and get milk and butter; it was only with the turf-firing cut on the common that they could smoke their bacon, hanging it in the wide chimneys over those old open hearths where none but such fuel could be used; and, again, it was only because they could get furze from the common to heat their bread ovens that it was worth their while to grow a little wheat at home and have it ground into flour for making bread. With the common, however, they could, and did, achieve all this. I am not dealing in supposition. I have mentioned nothing here that I have not learnt from men who remember the system still flourishing – men who in their boyhood took part in it, and can tell how the turfs were harvested, and how the pig-litter was got home and stacked in ricks; men who, if you lead them on, will talk of the cows they themselves watched over on the heath – two from this cottage, three from that one yonder, one more from Master Hack's, another couple from Trusler's, until they have numbered a score, perhaps, and have named a dozen old village names. It all actually happened. The whole system was 'in full swing' here, within living memory. But the very heart of it was the open common.

Accordingly, when the enclosure began to be a fact, when the cottager was left with nothing to depend upon save his garden alone, as a peasant he was a broken man – a peasant shut out from his countryside and cut off from his resources. True, he might still grow vegetables, and keep a pig or two, and provide himself with pork; but there was little else that he could do in the old way. It was out of the question to obtain most of his supplies by his own handiwork: they had to be procured, ready-made, from some other source. That source, I need hardly say, was a shop. So the once self-supporting cottager turned into a spender of money at the baker's, the coal-merchant's, the provision-dealer's; and, of course, needing to spend money, he needed first to get it.

GEORGE BOURNE

The Lay of the Labourer

A spade! a rake! a hoe!
　　A pickaxe, or a bill!
A hook to reap, or a scythe to mow,
　　A flail, or what ye will –
And here 's a ready hand
　　To ply the needful tool,
And skill'd enough, by lessons rough,
　　In Labour's rugged school.

To hedge, or dig the ditch,
　　To lop or fell the tree,
To lay the swarth on the sultry field,
　　Or plough the stubborn lea;
The harvest stack to bind,
　　The wheaten rick to thatch,
And never fear in my pouch to find
　　The tinder or the match.

To a flaming barn or farm
　　My fancies never roam;
The fire I yearn to kindle and burn
　　Is on the hearth of Home;
Where children huddle and crouch
　　Through dark long winter days,
Where starving children huddle and crouch,
　　To see the cheerful rays,
A-glowing on the haggard cheek,
　　And not in the haggard's blaze!

To Him who sends a drought
   To parch the fields forlorn,
The rain to flood the meadows with mud,
   The lights to blast the corn,
To Him I leave to guide
   The bolt in its crooked path.
To strike the miser's rick, and show
   The skies blood-red with wrath.

A spade! a rake! a hoe!
   A pickaxe, or a bill!
A hook to reap, or a scythe to mow,
   A flail, or what ye will –
The corn to thrash, or the hedge to plash,
   The market-team to drive,
Or mend the fence by the cover side,
   And leave the game alive.

Ay, only give me work,
   And then you need not fear
That I shall snare his worship's hare,
   Or kill his grace's deer;
Break into his lordship's house,
   To steal the plate so rich;
Or leave the yeoman that had a purse
   To welter in a ditch.

Wherever Nature needs
   Wherever Labour calls,
No job I'll shirk of the hardest work,
   To shun the workhouse walls;

Where savage laws begrudge
   The pauper babe its breath,
And doom a wife to a widow's life,
   Before her partner's death.

My only claim is this,
   With labour stiff and stark,
By lawful turn, my living to earn,
   Between the light and dark;
My daily bread, and nightly bed,
   My bacon, and drop of beer –
But all from the hand that holds the land,
   And none from the overseer!

No parish money, or loaf,
   No pauper badges for me,
A son of the soil, by right of toil
   Entitled to my fee.
No alms I ask, give me my task:
   Here are the arm, the leg,
The strength, the sinews of a Man,
   To work, and not to beg.

Still one of Adam's heirs,
   Though doom'd by chance of birth
To dress so mean, and to eat the lean
   Instead of the fat of the earth;
To make such humble meals
   As honest labour can,
A bone and a crust, with a grace to God,
   And little thanks to man!

A spade! a rake! a hoe!
   A pickaxe, or a bill!
A hook to reap, or a scythe to mow,
   A flail, or what ye will –
Whatever the tool to ply,
   Here is a willing drudge,
With muscle and limb, and woe to him
   Who does their pay begrudge!

Who every weekly score
   Docks labour's little mite,
Bestows on the poor at the temple door,
   But robb'd them over night.
The very shilling he hoped to save,
   As health and morals fail,
Shall visit me in the New Bastille,
   The Spital, or the Gaol!

THOMAS HOOD

12

I couldn't tell you how we do live; it's a mystery.

MRS WEST

Study No. XVIII – North Riding of Yorkshire

MAN, wife, five daughters, aged eight, seven, five, two, and one.

TOTAL WEEKLY EARNINGS OF FAMILY

	s.	d.
Man's wage	9	0
Perquisites –		
Man's board, say	8	0
	17	0

Extra earnings in the course of the year, £1.
Rent of cottage and garden, 1s. 11d. per week.

The Arthurs live in what it would perhaps be most correct to describe as a 'two-roomed cottage with extras'. There is a rough loft, used in cases of emergency by all the children, and always by the two elder children; there are a wash-house, and a kind of pantry-scullery occupied by the shoes of the family, an ancient bicycle, and the frame used by Mrs Arthur when she is making hearthrugs. The provisions, too, are kept there on the shelf.

But there are only two comfortable rooms – the kitchen and bedroom on the ground floor. Both are good-sized as cottage accommodation goes.

There is a bright fire in the living-room, but it is very obviously the abode of poverty. There is no carpet on the stone floor, but a good-sized hearthrug and a smaller rug, both of them made out of clippings by Mrs Arthur, and two small bits of sacking. The place is clean and fresh. The wall would do with a new paper – the last, as Mrs Arthur explains, having been put on when 'there weren't so many of 'em'. But it is not likely to get it. Four or five almanacs are hung up, and on the mantelpiece are two gaudy advertisements, duplicates of 'Price's Child's Night Lights', two old vases, a clock, and various tins. There are five wooden chairs, including a small high-chair, a stool, and a wooden cradle.

As for the bedroom, it is pretty fully occupied by the two large bedsteads in which five Arthurs are dispersed at nights – father, mother, and baby in one bed; two children, aged five and three, in the other. There is no carpet on the red-brick floor. A chest of drawers faces the beds.

The Arthurs have been married nine years, during which time Arthur has been working regularly winter and summer for one farmer, for 9s. a week, paid fortnightly, and his food. The food comprises three square meals, with bacon for breakfast and tea, or supper, at 6 p.m., and beef, or perhaps mutton, for dinner, with apple pies, dumplings, 'sad-cakes', or whatever it happens to be.

'Last year,' he says, 't' farmer offered me 16s. a week and to meat misel, but 'taint sie good as the 9s. and 'im meatin' me.'

Doubtless the family as a whole might profit better for a time by the 16s. a week; but here, as elsewhere, the health of the breadwinner must be the first consideration. Arthur works hard for his wage, from 6 a.m. to 6 p.m., and also on Sundays. He has an hour off for dinner, but hardly a quarter of an hour for breakfast. In the summer he has to milk twice a day, and 'fodder t' stock' at dinner-time. In the winter there is a sheepfold to look after, and Sunday is nearly as hard as any other day.

'It's bed and wark wi' Arthur, poor thing,' said a sympathetic villager. 'He's nobbut had three days holiday sen he were married. An', rightly speakin', that weren't holidays like; yah tahm was when he went to t' show for his maister, and t'other tahm he was ill i' bed. To be sewer he went to Pedley (the nearest market town) las' Soondah. That war marvellous! He milked before he set out to walk, and he got anuther man to fodder an' milk at neet.'

Arthur is well liked in the village. He is a steady, hard-working, pleasant-faced, stalwart fellow; but the hard life is telling on him, and he looks more weary than a man of thirty-one years should look. Sometimes, too, his voice has a despondent ring, even though the next moment he will laugh heartily at a droll speech from his wife or the children's pranks.

'The childer are fair crazed aboot their dad,' says Mrs Arthur. She is a small, fair, energetic, and somewhat combative woman, who works hard, even furiously, making, mending, washing, cleaning, and baking, but who is said by the neighbours to be 'not much good at plannin''. Her bill of fare is more uncertain than that of most of the villagers. Sometimes she bakes more bread and uses fewer vegetables; sometimes, especially when the grocer's bill is getting too far in arrears, she tries to dispense with bread and live on turnips and carrots or potatoes out of the large garden at which Arthur works in the long evenings.

The two quarrel sometimes, or, in a village parlance, 'turn dark tongues to each uther' – a proceeding which is not considered edifying for the children, who 'learn that kind of talk soon enough, without hearing it at home'. But they are sincerely attached to one another and to the little ones, who look happy, clean, and fairly healthy.

They regard church or chapel going as an expensive, even a prohibitive, luxury, which is apt to have a deteriorating effect on those who indulge in it. Mrs Arthur only the day before had been asked by a neighbour why she never attended any place of worship. 'I said to her, "No, I doant gan to chapel, no mair dis he, and we bean't no worse'n them as dea. There's sum on 'em as'll pray and talk good at chapel, an' they'll sit doon to sike a meal as *we* could niver set doon to, and then they'll 'unger t' stock. There's Redington; 'e's fair 'ungered three 'orses to death, and when t' next dees 'e'll 'appen ask some of they ministers to raht a letter for 'im an' go collectin' for anuther. But

Arthur, I'll say this for 'im, 'e'd sooner 'unger hissen than t'stock. No, we deant 'old with chapel going. 'Taint the cleas; I'd go as I am, if I *did* go. If fooaks wanted me any differ, they could take t' claes off their awn backs and gi' 'em to me to put on."'

So Mrs Arthur, in her most defiant spirit. But even the defiance has an undercurrent of strained anxiety. In spite of the regularity of the pay, such as it is, and the kindliness of neighbours, and the large garden, with its couple of fruit trees and ample supply of vegetables, the life is hard – almost impossible. Only the other day she broke out to a neighbour as poor as herself. 'I's sewer money, it seems to awnt me day and neet. I cawn't reest for it; I doan't know t' reason on't. If it wasn't for t' wark I should go all wrang. I dean't like to be owing; I'd pay to t' last awpenny, look ye, and I dean't know 'ow to live any differ. I niver gies t' bairns a awpenny. I niver allows 'em to go for goodies – if I niver starts 'em they'll niver want. If they iver has a farden it's what other fooaks gi'es 'em, an' often I takes that frae 'em. I cawn't do no mair'n I can, and yet I disn't sleep for troublin'. Last neet I was out o'bed four times with t' lail 'un, an' then I sat ower on t' bed ruing. An' I had a good rue, and I felt a bit better.

'But I isn't a rogue, look yer, an' if I had t' money I wadn't get things wi'out payin'. I ain't bowt meat nor bacon for weeks an' weeks. I get a bit o' lard and meeak some sad-cakes for t' childer an' mysen. I feel as if I mun hae sumethin' I can eat, an' it saves t' butter. *He* niver bites at home – nobbut a drink o' tea – he'd think it would be takkin' it oot of our mooths. But t' kids is that 'ungry, I tell yer, they'd eat me up if I was meat an' bread an' stuff – they would, I'se sewer! I told a man I owes two shillings would 'e take five kids instead. But he said he niver took 'em by less ner t' awf-dozen!'

Mrs Arthur's debts, when taken together, perhaps do not seem so appalling. There is £1, 1s. 6d. for shoes, at three different shops within a radius of six miles, about 5s. at one grocer's and about 4s. at another. There is the 2s. above mentioned, incurred for towels, bought in before the last confinement. And there are doctor's bills amounting to 26s. The rent book is clear. But these debts are making an old woman of Mrs Arthur, though she is only twenty-six. She is overworked and underfed – and they are all the latter, even the baby.

'*That* little customer wants sarvin' three times a day wi' bried an' milk an' sugar; an' she could eat more – they all could.'

The harvest money is only £1, and that is the one extra allowed. This year part of it was mortgaged to the farmer for insurance and the weekly half-pound of butter. The rest wiped off some arrears, but not the whole. Twelve shillings went for rent. Arthur's master is not liberal with gifts, although last year he did give him 'a glazy coat' (mackintosh) for shepherding.

They have only other people's 'cast-offs' to rely upon in the matter of clothing.

'If we didn't hae cleas given, we suld hae to black oorsels ower an' go naykt,' says Mrs Arthur.

Last week her mother had given her a pound of curds, and this week her brother – both living in a town ten miles away – gave her 2s. But that is the first money gift she has had since her confinement a year ago. A lady at a distance, who stayed at the village last year, has paid for a pint of milk a day for her ever since. Sometimes the children get 'bits' given, but such gifts are quite incalculable.

'They 'ev 'ad nowt lately.'

A neighbour, however, brought her a cod's head this week.

Her mother cannot help her much, as the father only earns 15s. a week as a gate opener on the railway. He has five to keep, and the rent is £12 a year.

There is a deficiency of 34 per cent of protein in this family's dietary, and of 30 per cent of energy value. One-sixteenth of the food consumed is home produce, and one-fifth is given.

	s.	d.		s.	d.
1 lb sugar	0	2	Soap, soda	0	2
½ lb butter	0	6½	Matches	0	0½
1 cwt coal	1	3	Paraffin	0	1½
¼ lb tea	0	4½	Baking powder	0	1¼
1 lb treacle	0	2½	¼ lb ground rice	0	0¾
1½ stones flour	2	7½	Rent (weekly)	1	11
2 oz yeast	0	1½	Tobacco	0	5½
Salt	0	0½	Insurance	0	4
¾ lb lard	0	5½		9	0

HOME PRODUCE CONSUMED DURING THE WEEK

8 lbs potatoes   7½ lbs turnips

GIFTS CONSUMED DURING THE WEEK

¼ lb butter   7 pints whole milk
1 lb curds   Cod's head

MENU OF MEALS PROVIDED DURING THE WEEK

	BREAKFAST	DINNER	TEA	SUPPER
SUN.	Tea with milk (no sugar), sad-cakes, cheesecake, bread and butter.	Turnips and potatoes.	Tea and milk, curd cheese-cake.	Tea, bread and butter, sad-cake.
MON.	Tea and milk, bread and butter, cheesecake.	Turnips and potatoes.	Tea and milk, bread and butter, sad-cakes, cheesecake.	Tea, bread and butter, cheesecake.
TUES.	Bread and treacle, tea with milk, cheesecake.	Tea, bread and treacle.	Tea, sad-cake and treacle, cheesecake.	Tea, bread and treacle.

WED.	Tea, bread and treacle, sad-cake and treacle.	Turnips and potatoes.	Tea, bread and treacle.	Tea, bit of dry sad-cake.
THUR.	Tea, milk-powder cakes.	Cod's head and pota-toes.	Tea, dry powder cakes.	Tea.
FRI.	Tea and cakes with butter.	Sad-cakes with butter, tea.	Tea and milk, hot sad-cake and cheese-cake.	None.
SAT.	Tea and milk, bread and treacle, cheesecake.	Sad-cakes and treacle, tea.	Tea, bread and treacle, curd cheese-cake.	Tea, bread and butter.

On about two days in the week the woman and the little girl have tea and bread and butter between breakfast and dinner.

The children have supper one day in the week (Sunday). The man generally has merely a drink of tea at supper-time, but on Sundays a piece of bread and butter also. The woman has supper fairly regularly.

B. S. ROWNTREE AND M. KENDALL

14

I F they eat jam, it includes more bread – they eats more! If I cut a slice of bread and put margarine on it, may be two slices will do; but if I put jam on it, it'll be, 'Mummy, give me another slice.' That's my conclusion about jam.

. . . People think we're well off because we've the house free. What I say to 'em is, 'We can't eat the house.'

MRS BELL

'You hold the plough, you say; how old are you?'

'I bees sixteen a'most.'

'What wages have you?'

'Three shillin' a-week.'

'Three shillings! Have you nothing else? Don't you get victuals, or part of them, from your master?'

'No, I buys them all.'

'All out of three shillings?'

'Ees, and buys my clothes out of that.'

'And what do you buy to eat?'

'Buy to eat! Why, I buys bread and lard.'

'Do you eat bread and lard always? What have you for breakfast?'

'What have I for breakfast? Why, bread and lard.'

'And what for dinner?'

'Bread and lard.'

'What for supper, the same?'

'Ees, the same for supper – bread and lard.'

'It seems to be always bread and lard, have you no boiled bacon and vegetables?'

'No, there be no place to boil 'em; no time to boil 'em; none to boil.'

'Have you never a hot dinner nor supper; don't you get potatoes?'

'Ees, potatoes, an we pay for 'em. Master lets us boil 'em once a-week an we like.'

'And what do you eat to them; bacon?'

'No.'

'What then?'

'Lard; never has nothing but lard.'

'Can't you boil potatoes or cook your victuals any day you choose?'

'No; has no fire.'

'Have you no fire to warm you in cold weather?'

'No, we never has fire.'

'Where do you go in the winter evenings?'

'To bed, when it be time; an it ben't time, we goes to some of the housen as be round about.'

'To the firesides of some of the cottagers, I suppose?'

'Ees, an we can get.'

'What if you cannot get; do you go into the farm-house?'

'No, mustn't; never goes nowhere but to bed an it be very cold.'

'Where is your bed?'

'In the *tollit*' (stable loft).

'How many of you sleep there?'

'All on us as be hired.'

'How many are hired?'

'Four last year, five this.'

'Does any one make your beds for you?'

'No, we make 'em ourselves.'

'Who washes your sheets?'

'Who washes 'em?'

'Yes; they *are* washed, I suppose?'

'No, they ben't.'

'What! never washed? Do you mean to say you don't have your sheets washed?'

'No, never since I comed.'

'When did you come?'

'Last Michaelmas.'

'Were your bedclothes clean then?'

'I dare say they was.'

'And don't you know how long they are to serve until they are changed again?'

'To Michaelmas, I hear tell.'

'So one change of bedclothes serves a year! Don't you find your bed disagreeable?'

'Do I! I bees too sleepy. I never knows nought of it, only that I has to get up afore I be awake, and never get into it afore I be a'most asleep. I be up at four, and ben't done work afore eight at night.'

'You don't go so long at the plough as that?'

'No; but master be always having summat for we to do as be hired; we be always at summat.'

A. SOMERVILLE

16

MEN used to start the day on a breakfast of bread soaked in hot water, salted and peppered. Bread and onions had been eaten in the fields at dinner-time. A man's wage would not buy bread for a family, let alone any meat. 'No, nor it wun't now', Jasper said, 'if there be any childer.' Someone told of an occasion when a family of parents and nine children had shared a single bloater at Sunday dinner. Cabbage had been a great standby. The young children, they said, had lived on cabbage and lard. 'My old 'ooman', said one of them, 'says cabbage killed many a babby, but kept the next biggest alive.' Now in the seventies the men brought a bit of cheese as well as an onion. When they ate at home they might have suet pudding with scraps of bacon rolled in it and mushrooms, too, once or twice a year, and then it was the richest of dishes. Usually this talk was cheerful; times were not so bad as they had been, but sometimes a darker spirit ruled. Life was hard laabour abroad, squalling babbies at whum, and the workus at last. The workus was hell, but a cold un. And all, mark you, in a land of plenty. There was nothing to live for.

M. K. ASHBY

17

As a man, he is usually strongly built, broad-shouldered, and massive in frame, but his appearance is spoilt by the clumsiness of his walk and the want of grace in his movements. Though quite as large in muscle, it is very doubtful if he possesses the strength of the seamen who may be seen lounging about the ports. There is a want of firmness, a certain disjointed style, about his limbs, and the muscles themselves have not the hardness and tension of the sailor's. The labourer's muscle is that of a cart-horse, his motions lumbering and slow. His style of walk is caused by following the plough in early childhood, when the weak limbs find it a hard labour to pull the heavy nailed boots from the thick clay soil. Ever afterwards he walks as if it were an exertion to lift his legs. His food may, perhaps, have something to do with the deadened slowness which seems to pervade everything he does – there seems a lack of vitality about him. It consists chiefly of bread and cheese, with bacon twice or thrice a week, varied with onions, and if he be a milker (on some farms) with a good 'tuck-out' at his employer's expense on Sundays. On ordinary days he dines at the fashionable hour of six or seven in the evening – that is, about that time his cottage scents the road with a powerful odour of boiled cabbage, of which he eats an immense quantity. Vegetables are his luxuries . . .

RICHARD JEFFERIES

'Is there anything you can fancy that you would like to eat?' I once said to an old labouring man, who was in his last illness, and who had refused all the food his wife had offered him. 'No.' he answered, 'I've never been used to nothing but common victual, and I can't eat that.'

GEORGE ELIOT

19

In winter in the 'eighties the youths and big boys of the hamlet would go out on dark nights 'spadgering'. For this a large net upon four poles was carried; two bearers going on one side of a hedge and two on the other. When they came to a spot where a flock of sparrows or other small birds was roosting, the net was dropped over the hedge and drawn tight and the birds enclosed were slaughtered by lantern light. One boy would often bring home as many as twenty sparrows, which his mother would pluck and make into a pudding. A small number of birds, or a single bird, would be toasted in front of the fire.

FLORA THOMPSON

THE robin and the wren
　　Are God Almighty's cock and hen
The martin and the swallow
Are God Almighty's bow and arrow.

TRADITIONAL

21

Mutton Pie

COME all you jolly lads if you want to learn to plough,
　Go to Yorkie Watson, he'll show you how;
He's got four 'osses and they're all very thin
'Cause he doesn't put much hay in the bin.
To me whack fol the diddle ol the day,
To me whack fol the diddle ol the day.

Now our owd mester he went to the fair,
Bought four 'osses and yan were a mare;
Yan were blin' and t'other couldn't see,
And t'other 'ad 'is 'ead where 'is arse ought to be.
To me whack fol the diddle, etc.

Now our owd missis thinks she's giving you a treat,
Bakes such pies aren't fit to eat;
There's pies made of iron and cakes made o' clay,
Rattlin' in your belly for a month and a day.
To me whack fol the diddle, etc.

Our owd missis 'as a mate called Alice,
Thowt she were fit to live in a palace,
Live in a palace and be like a queen:
I'm damned if she were fit to be seen.
To me whack fol the diddle, etc.

Well, our owd mester to us did say:
'There's a yowe been dead for a month and a day;
Fetch 'er up, Bullocky, fetch 'er up, Sly,
We'll mek our lads some rare mutton pie.'
To me whack fol the diddle, etc.

So they fetched th'owd yowe and laid her on t' table
To mek 'em a pie as fast as they were able;
There was maggots by the hundreds, thousands, millions
   thick,
Bullocky were wallockin' 'em off wi' a stick.
To me whack fol the diddle, etc.

So come all you jolly fellows if you want to learn to plough,
Go to Yorkie Watson, he'll show you how;
He'll show you how, me boys, I've heard say,
Wants you to plough four acre a day.
To me whack fol the diddle, etc.

TRADITIONAL

22

THERE were usually three or four ploughs to a field, each of
them drawn by a team of three horses, with a boy at the
head of the leader and the ploughman behind at the shafts. All

day, up and down they would go, ribbing the pale stubble with stripes of dark furrows, which, as the day advanced, would get wider and nearer together, until, at length, the whole field lay a rich velvety plum-colour.

Each plough had its following of rooks, searching the clods with sidelong glances for worms and grubs. Little hedgerow birds flitted hither and thither, intent upon getting their tiny share of whatever was going. Sheep, penned in a neighbouring field, bleated complainingly; and above the ma-a-ing and cawing and twittering rose the immemorial cries of the landworker: 'Wert up!' 'Who-o-o-a!' 'Go it, Poppet!' 'Go it, Lightfoot!' 'Boo-oy, be you deaf, or be you hard of hearin', dang ye!'

After the plough had done its part, the horse-drawn roller was used to break down the clods; then the harrow to comb out and leave in neat piles the weeds and the twitch grass which infested those fields, to be fired later and fill the air with the light blue haze and the scent that can haunt for a lifetime. Then seed was sown, crops were thinned out and hoed and, in time, mown, and the whole process began again.

FLORA THOMPSON

23

Ox Plough Song

COME all you sweet charmers, come give me choice,
    For there's nothing to compare with a ploughboy's voice,
For to hear the little ploughboy singing so sweet,
Makes the hills and the valleys around us to meet.
For 'tis hark the little ploughboy gets up in the morn,
Whoop along, jump along,

Here drives the ploughboy with Spark and Beauty Berry,
Good luck Speedwell, Cherry,
For it's Whoop a long,
For we are the lads that can keep along the plough,
For we are the lads that can keep along the plough.

In the heat of the day what a little we can do,
We lay by the plough for an hour or two,
On the banks of sweet violets where we take our rest,
Where the cool, stormy winds blow around us so fast.
For 'tis hark the little ploughboy, etc.

If the farmer hath no corn, no corn can he sow,
Then the miller hath no work for his mill also,
And the baker hath no bread for the poor to provide,
If the plough should stand still we should all starve alive.
For 'tis hark the little ploughboy, etc.

And now to conclude, my song must here have an end,
I hope the little ploughboy won't ever want a friend,
Here's health unto the ploughboy and merry we'll be,
Here's health unto the ploughboy and God Save the King.
For 'tis hark the little ploughboy, etc.

TRADITIONAL

Harry Ploughman

Hard as hurdle arms, with a broth of goldish flue
    Breathed round; the rack of ribs; the scooped flank; lank
Rope-over thigh; knee-nave; and barrelled shank —
        Head and foot, shoulder and shank —
By a grey eye's heed steered well, one crew, fall to;
Stand at stress. Each limb's barrowy brawn, his thew
That onewhere curded, onewhere sucked or sank —
        Soared or sank —,
Though as a beechbole firm, finds his, as at a roll-call, rank
And features, in flesh, what deed he each must do —
        His sinew-service where do.

He leans to it, Harry bends, look. Back, elbow, and liquid waist
In him, all quail to the wallowing o' the plough: 's cheek
    crimsons; curls
Wag or crossbridle, in a wind lifted, windlaced —
        See his wind- lilylocks -laced;
Churlsgrace, too, child of Amansstrength, how it hangs or hurls
Them — broad in bluffhide his frowning feet lashed! raced
With, along them, cragiron under and cold furls —
        With-a-fountain's shining-shot furls.

GERARD MANLEY HOPKINS

B<small>UT</small>, unassisted through each toilsome day,
   With smiling brow the plowman cleaves his way,
Draws his fresh parallels, and wid'ning still,
Treads slow the heavy dale, or climbs the hill:
Strong on the wing his busy followers play,
Where writhing earth-worms meet th' unwelcome day;
Till all is chang'd, and hill and level down
Assume a livery of sober brown:
Again disturb'd, when Giles with wearying strides
From ridge to ridge the ponderous harrow guides;
His heels deep sinking every step he goes,
Till dirt usurp the empire of his shoes.

ROBERT BLOOMFIELD

26

A ploughman's voice, a clink of chain,
   Slow hoofs, and harness under strain,
Up the slow slope a team came bowing,
Old Callow at his autumn ploughing,
Old Callow, stooped above the hales,
Ploughing the stubble into wales;
His grave eyes looking straight ahead,
Shearing a long straight furrow red;
His plough-foot high to give it earth
To bring new food for men to birth.

*

Slow up the hill the plough team plod,
Old Callow at the task of God,
Helped by man's wit, helped by the brute
Turning a stubborn clay to fruit,
His eyes for ever on some sign
To help him plough a perfect line.
At top of rise the plough team stopped,
The fore-horse bent his head and cropped.
Then the chains chack, the brasses jingle,
The lean reins gather through the cringle,
The figures move against the sky,
The clay wave breaks as they go by.

JOHN MASEFIELD

27

The Ploughboy

COME all you jolly ploughboys, come listen to my lays,
  And join with me in chorus, I'll sing the ploughboy's
praise;
My song is of the ploughboy's fame, and unto you I'll relate
the same;
He whistles, sings and drives his team, the brave ploughing
boy.

So early in the morning, the ploughboy he is seen;
He hastens to the stable, his horses for to clean.
Their manes and tails he will comb straight, with chaff and
corn he does them bait,
Then he'll endeavour to plough straight, the brave ploughing
boy.

Now all things being ready, and the harness that's put to,
All with a shining countenance his work he will pursue.
The small birds sing on every tree, the cuckoo joins in
    harmony
To welcome us as you may say, the brave ploughing boy.

So early in the morning, to harrow, plough and sow –
And with a gentle cast, my boys, we'll give the corn a throw,
Which makes the vallies thick to stand with corn to fill the
    reaper's hand:
All this, you well may understand, comes from the ploughing
    boy.

Now the corn it is a-growing, and seed time that's all o'er,
Our master he does welcome us and unlocks the cellar door;
With cake and ale we have our fill because we've done our
    work so well,
There's none here can excel the skill of a brave ploughing boy.

Now the corn it is a-growing, the fields look fresh and gay,
The cheerful lads come in to mow, whilst damsels make the
    hay;
The ears of corn they now appear, and peace and plenty
    crowns the year,
So we'll be merry whilst we are here and drink to the brave
    ploughing boy.

TRADITIONAL

Children's Song on Valentine's Day, at Eastleach

Mornty, Mornty, Valentine!
 Blow the oats against the wind,
We are ragged and you are fine,
So please to give us a Valentine.

TRADITIONAL

29

THE rick was unhaled by full daylight; the men then took their places, the women mounted, and the work began. Farmer Groby – or, as they called him, 'he' – had arrived ere this, and by his orders Tess was placed on the platform of the machine, close to the man who fed it, her business being to untie every sheaf of corn handed on to her by Izz Huett, who stood next, but on the rick; so that the feeder could seize it and spread it over the revolving drum, which whisked out every grain in one moment.

They were soon in full progress, after a preparatory hitch or two, which rejoiced the hearts of those who hated machinery. The work sped on till breakfast-time, when the thresher was stopped for half an hour; and on starting again after the meal the whole supplementary strength of the farm was thrown into the labour of constructing the straw-rick, which began to grow beside the stack of corn. A hasty lunch was eaten as they stood, without leaving their positions, and then another couple of hours brought them near to dinner-time; the inexorable wheels continuing to spin, and the penetrating hum of the thresher to thrill to the very marrow all who were near the revolving wire-cage.

The old men on the rising straw-rick talked of the past days when they had been accustomed to thresh with flails on the oaken barn-floor; when everything, even to winnowing, was effected by hand-labour, which, to their thinking, though slow, produced better results. Those, too, on the corn-rick talked a little; but the perspiring ones at the machine, including Tess, could not lighten their duties by the exchange of many words. It was the ceaselessness of the work which tried her so severely, and began to make her wish that she had never come to Flintcomb-Ash. The women on the corn-rick – Marian, who was one of them, in particular – could stop to drink ale or cold tea from the flagon now and then, or to exchange a few gossiping remarks while they wiped their faces or cleared the fragments of straw and husk from their clothing; but for Tess there was no respite; for, as the drum never stopped, the man who fed it could not stop, and she, who had to supply the man with untied sheaves, could not stop either, unless Marian changed places with her, which she sometimes did for half an hour in spite of Groby's objection that she was too slow-handed for a feeder.

THOMAS HARDY

30

THEY called them the 'Good Old Days'. Of course, only ignorant people thought that. Just you imagine, a boy, eleven or twelve years of age, getting up in the morning; walking three miles to where the threshing tackle was. He'd be at work in the dust and that, all day. What did he get? Four pence a day. If you see any old photographs of threshing tackle, you'll see there is generally the beer bottle well in the foreground. Well! that beer bottle earned the boy more than he earned in wages, because the stacks were full of rats and the farmers always paid a penny a tail, for every tail handed in. The men used to take it out in beer. All the money collected was put in what they called the beer bottle. The boys used to take theirs out in cash. A boy's weekly wage was two bob a week. Very often he'd earned three-and-six or four bob a week rat-tail money, because the stacks were smothered with rats and it paid them to kill 'em. Well! there were only a few of them to share it.

The old chap who fed the threshing machine had cut off the tails with his pocket knife; a few seconds later he'd open his dinner basket; pull out his bread-and-cheese and that; out with his pocket knife, and Ha! ha! ha! But it was all killing work. You see, a man never got a full wage of two shillings a day until he could carry corn all day. That was, carrying an eighteen [stones] sack of corn from the threshing tackle to the barn. Till he could do that he'd have one day trying of it. See? A lad of seventeen was classed as a three-quarter man. He got eight shillings a week. Well! to prove he was a three-quarter man, he'd have to spend all day, from half-past six in the morning till half-past five at night, carrying sacks of oats from the threshing machine – about a hundred yards – to the barn. Those sacks weighed twelve stones. I know what I'm talking about, because I've done the damn thing.

W. H. BARRETT

'HAVE you ever done any threshing?' I replied, 'No, Sir; I have not.' 'Very well then,' he says, 'your mates have been telling me that I have paid you more than you have earned, and they are the same age as you; so unless you are willing to do some threshing I am afraid I shall not be able to find you anything to do.' I replied, 'I have no flail.' He said, 'I cannot help that.' I then said, 'I will try and get one ready.'

When I reached home I told father what had been said. Father replied, 'Never mind, do your best; prove to him that you are not afraid of work.' So father and I spent the whole of that evening in preparing for the following Monday morning. Father got the flail ready; I went to the harness-maker's for a swindgel cap. This is the beater that knocks out the corn. Then to the carpenter's for to get a rake; this was to separate the cavings from the corn. So on the Monday morning at 6 a.m. I presented myself at the farm, armed with my flail, rake, and fork. The bailiff was surprised, and said, 'I thought you said you had not got a flail?' I replied, 'More I had not, but it does not take long to get a stick and a half. What is it you want me to do?' He replied, 'Here, take this key and start to thresh the barn of barley at Bush Barn (the name of the farm), and mind you thresh it clean; then I shall see if you are a man.' I said, 'How am I to do it? By the day, or take it?' He said, 'Take it, of course; I told you this [was] to try you.' 'Very well,' I says. 'What am I to have per quarter? We may as well start plain.' He replied, 'The same as I pay Groves, 2s. 6d. per quarter.' To this I agreed; and with this said I at once rounded to my work.

Now, here I wish to explain that at this period most of the barley grown was threshed by the flail. Certain men went into the barns after harvest, and many were thus employed until late in the spring; so on a farm growing forty or fifty acres of barley, two men would be at this work, week in and week out, while another batch would be doing such work as I have described in the earlier pages. These were liable to loss of time in bad weather, whereas those in the barns need never lose any time.

When I reached my barn I at once found out how many rows of barley it was possible to lay out for threshing at a time. The next thing I did was to time myself – how long it took me to thresh it. Then I estimated how much thereby I got in each lot I threshed. So at the end of each day I thought I had some idea of how much barley I was threshing. After two or three days' work I had gained a bit more room. I also tried to do a few more rows daily, as I got more used to the work. After this I improved my methods and made great progress. I was rather anxious to see how the bailiff would frame when he came to inspect the straw, to see if I had threshed all the corn off of it. Now, to thresh grain clean there is only one way. There are so many inches of space across the floor whereon is laid the grain. A man giving fifty or sixty blows where only one or two are necessary, and omitting to administer the blows where necessary, cannot thresh all the grain off; and, not only that, he is, as it were, beating air. I wanted to get a 'bull's-eye' each stroke; so I methodically began at one end of the row and slowly thrashed from one end to the other, then back again; then turn up the edge the same as a woman doing needlework turns up the hem; then, after this was done, I turned the row right over and repeated the dose, and so I finished off the batch, and so on. When the bailiff come to inspect the straw he appeared satisfied. He said, 'Yes, this will do; mind and get all the barley out of the cavings as well.' I said, 'I will do my best.' So on the first Saturday night I locked up the barn and went to receive my first payment. The bailiff says, 'How much do you want to draw?' I replied, 'Fifteen shillings.' 'Fifteen shillings!' he exclaimed. 'Why that's more than Groves draws.' I said, 'Well, I cannot help that; you said I was to do what I could.' He then said, 'If you overdraw you will have to repay it.' I said, 'Certainly, I will.' After this I put every ounce of energy I could into it; hung my watch by the side of the barn, and worked against time, and continued to draw my money, as I had begun. Why I did this was, had I only drawn the same amount as I had been taking when working by the day I should not have received the amount I was earning. I was packing my straw up daily, so it could be seen as often as they chose, whereas when the man Groves was threshing on another farm his straw and caving were thrown into the yard, where there were a hundred hungry pigs, and if there was any barley left in this or in the cavings these pigs found it. There was at one end of this barn a low end; so this I utilized to store my corn, and thus when the time came to dress up this ready for market I was pleased to find I had under-estimated my quantities. This was what I was striving for. As I was busy as a bee, this seemed one of the shortest winters I ever experienced, and at the end of the threshing I had a sum to receive that I took in gold. If ever there was anyone proud of any achievement, that was me. 'Something accomplished, something done.'

ISAAC MEAD

32

THE thresher dull as winter days
     And lost to all that spring displays
Still mid his barn dust forcd to stand
Swings his frail round wi weary hand

JOHN CLARE

Pace Egg Song – Chipping

There's three or four jolly lads all in a row,
 We've come a-pace-egging we'll have you to know,
Put your hand in your pocket and pull out your purse,
And give us a trifle, you'll ne'er be no worse.
Singing fol de roll the day,
Fol the day, fol the day rule I day.

The first that comes in is Lord Nelson, you see,
With a bunch of blue ribbon tied down to his knee,
And a star on his breast like silver doth shine,
And we hope yow'll remember it's pace-egging time.
Singing fol de roll the day, etc.

The next that comes in is Owd Nan in her rags,
She's as ragg'd as a sheep and as black as a crow,
She's as ragg'd as a sheep and as black as a crow,
And she will follow after wherever we go.
Singing fol de roll the day, etc.

So go down in your cellar and bring up some beer,
And we'll drink your good health and wish you much cheer,
We'll drink your good health and wish you much cheer,
And we'll come no more here until the next year.
Singing fol de roll the day, etc.

TRADITIONAL

T HE people were at work ploughing, harrowing, and sowing; lasses spreading dung, a dog's barking now and then,
cocks crowing, birds twittering, the snow in patches at the top of
the highest hills, yellow palms, purple and green twigs on the
birches, ashes with their glittering spikes quite bare. The
hawthorn a bright green, with black stems under the oak. The
moss of the oak glossy. We then went on, passed two sisters at
work (*they first passed us*), one with two pitchforks in her hand, the
other held a spade. We had some talk with them. They laughed
aloud after we were gone, perhaps half in wantonness, half
boldness.

DOROTHY WORDSWORTH

35
The Sower's Song

N ow hands to seed-sheet, boys!
We step and we cast; old Time's on wing,
And would ye partake of Harvest's joys,
The corn must be sown in Spring.
Fall gently and still, good corn,
Lie warm in thy earthy bed;
And stand so yellow some morn,
For beast and man must be fed.

Old Earth is a pleasure to see
In sunshiny cloak of red and green;

The furrow lies fresh: this Year will be
As Years that are past have been.
Fall gently, etc.

Old Mother, receive this corn,
The son of Six Thousand golden sires:
All these on thy kindly breast were born;
One more thy poor child requires.
Fall gently, etc.

Now steady and sure again,
And measure of stroke and step we keep;
Thus up and thus down we cast our grain:
Sow well, and you gladly reap.
Fall gently, etc.

THOMAS CARLYLE

36

The sower striding oer his dirty way
   Sinks anckle deep in pudgy sloughs and clay
And oer his heavy hopper stoutly leans
Strewing wi swinging arms the pattering beans
Which soon as aprils milder weather gleams
Will shoot up green between the furroed seams

JOHN CLARE

One for the mouse, one for the crow,
One to rot and one to grow.

TRADITIONAL

38

May Song of the Children at Shilton

GOOD morning, ladies and gentlemen, it is the first of May,
And we are come to garlanding because it is new May
Day;
A bunch of flowers we have brought you, and at your door we
stay,
So please to give us what you can, and then we'll go away.

TRADITIONAL

The Story of My Life

WHEN · I · WAS · A · LITTEL · GIRL ·
THE · TROUTH · TO · YOU · I · TELL ·
I · LIVED · WITH · MY · DEAR ·
FRENS · A · TOME · THEY ·
KEAP · A · LITTEL · COW · AND ·
I · CANNOT · TELL · YOU ·
HOW · I · IN · JOYED · A · RON ·
TO · FICH · HER · HOME ·

YES · I · LIVED · WITH · MY ·
DEAR · FRENS · SO · KIND ·
THEN · THE · COW · WENT ·
OUT · TO · GRASS · AND ·
THE · TIME · SO · MERRELY ·
PAST · WHEN · I · WENT ·
IN · THE · COMMON ·
HER · TO · FIND ·

MY · FATHER · WHENT · A · WAY ·
TO · HES · LABOUR · ALL · THE · DAY ·
WHILE · MY · MOTHER · ALL · HER ·
WORK · DID · DO · A · TOME · AND ·
THE · PUDING · WAS · SO · NIES ·
THAT · WAS · MEAD · WITH ·
MILK · AND · RICE · DOUNT · YOU ·
THINK · THAT · I · HAD · A · GOOD · HOME ·

IT · WAS · THEN · A · GOOD · LIVING ·
THEY · DID · GET · AND · IT · WAS ·
BY · THE · SEET · OF · THER ·

BROW · MY · KIND · FRINES ·
I · NEVER · CAN · FORGET ·
AND · IT · WAS · WHEN · THY ·
KEEP · THAT · LITTEL · COW ·

IT · WAS · THEN · I · LIVED · HAPPY ·
AND · FREE · THEN · THE ·
BUTTER · WAS · SENT · TO ·
SHOP · AND · SOME · OTHER ·
GOODS · WE · GOT · THE · TIME ·
AGINE · I · NEVER · MORE ·
SHELL · SEE ·

THEN · SOME · PIGS · THEY · DID ·
KEEP · TO · MAKE · THER · OWN ·
MEAT · AND · THERE · GARDENES ·
WELL · STORED · WITH · CORN ·
THEY · MADE · THER · OWN ·
BRED · WITH · THER · OWN ·
GROWN · WETE · TWAS · BEFOR ·
MY · YOUNGS · SISTER · WAS · BORN ·

AND · THEN · MY · FATHER · THOUGHT ·
HE · WOLD · BELD · A · LITTEL ·
COT · AND · TO · WHICH · THEN ·
HE · SOON · DID · BEGIN · BUT ·
MY · FATHERS · HALTH · DID ·
FEAIL · AND · IT · BLUE · A · DIFFERENT ·
GALE · BEFORE · HE · GOT · IT ·
REDEY · TO · LIVE · IN ·

MY · MOTHER · WAS · SO · KIND ·
AND · SHE · NEVER · HAD · A ·
MIND · A · WAY · THEN · A ·

63

GOSPING · TO · ROME · SHE ·
WORKED · WITH · ALL · HER · MIGHT ·
AND · IT · WAS · HER ·
HARTS · DELIGHT · TO · BE · WITH ·
HER · CHILDRING · AT · TOME ·

MY · FATHER · SAID · ONE · DAY ·
HE · WAS · GOING · A · LITTLE · WAY ·
I · MOST · STAY · AT · TOME · HE · WOLD ·
NOT · BE · LONG · BUT · I · NEW ·
THAT · HE · WAS · WEKE · AND · I ·
AFTER · HIM · DID · CREP · FOR ·
FEAR · HE · WOLD · FOLE · IN · TO ·
THE · POOND ·

I · DHUGED · HIM · A · LONG · TILL ·
MY · MOTHER · HE · MAT · WILE ·
THE · LITTLE · ONES · I · LEFT ·
THEM · ALONE · SHE · SAID · MY ·
DEAREST · DEAR · HOW · COULD ·
YOU · WONDER · HEAR ·
I · AM · A · FREAD · THAT · YOU ·
NEVER · WILL · GET · HOME ·

AND · THEN · MY · MOTHER · SEAD ·
YOUR · TIRED · I · AM · AFREAD ·
TO · CARRY · YOU · IT · IS · MY ·
GOOD · WILL · NOW · YOU ·
MAY · THINK · IT · QUER · BUT ·
AS · TRUE · AS · I · AM · HERE ·
SHE · CARRIED · HIM · ON · HER ·
BACK · UP · THE · HILL ·

THEN · MY · FATHER · DIED ·
AND · WE · ALL · BETTERLY · CRID ·
BUT · MY · MOTHER · SED · IT · IS · THE ·
LORDS · WILL · SO · MY · BROTHER ·
SED · IEL · WORK · THEN · MY ·
FATHERS · PLES · TO · FELL ·
SO · A · WEY · THEN · WE · WENT ·
LIKE · TO · DOVES · HAPPY · AS ·
THE · KING · AND · QUIN ·
OF · IN · THE · MORNING · AT ·
6 · AND · HOME · AT · NIGHT · AT · 9 ·

                                    ANON.

JOHN BRUDENELL, labourer. – I have worked here (Irchester) for eleven years. I have only one son, aged 30. There used to be no school here. I used to teach them in the winter. They did not know where to go, and they wanted some learning, so I said, 'I'll teach you.' That was 28 years ago. About six came to my cottage to be taught. That went on for two winters. I took it up again about three years since, because there was no school. The boys' friends asked me. I let them come to my house. Seventeen was the most I had; I had no room for more. I might have had many more if I had had room. They paid me 1d. per week and found their own lights. They each brought a candle in turn. I taught them to read, write, and spell. They came very regularly for about four months. They were all boys. I took it up like out of pity for them. Their friends wanted them to learn. They used to come from 7 to 8. They got on uncommon well some on 'em. Many of them did not know how to make a stroke when they came, and could write their names fair when they left. There are a good many now who want to learn, but they don't like to go to the school, because there are not enough people to teach 'em. A man cannot manage more than a score; 30 or 40 go to the night school now. I think it would be a very good thing if a law said you shall not send your boy to work unless he can read and write. It would sometimes be a hardship on the families, but I think he could learn enough between the ages of 7 and 10. At the age of 6 or 7 a child can take care of the younger children, so that the mother can go about the housework. It would be rather inconvenient if the child were taken away at that age. I believe much of the children's time is wasted; that is because they ain't made to go to school.

THE school in our village was one of the parson kind, but luckily for us youngsters it was a downright good one. For that we had to thank our master; it was entirely owing to him. I can truthfully say that our master all those years ago was, master for master, a better one than the man they have there now. Our man was sensible and practical above the common, and he had the true interests of his scholars at heart. He knew how important it was that during the very few years of schooling we could have, we should be taught what would prove of most use to us in everyday life. He flatly refused to waste his time and ours over the catechism and other useless educational lumber of the same sort, to the exclusion of what it was so much more necessary for us to know. He was determined that he would make boys fit to do something to earn their living when they left school; and he stuck manfully to that determination. He was as excellent a teacher as a poor boy could wish to meet with, and I shall never forget what I owe to him. It would have been difficult to beat him at reading, writing, spelling, arithmetic, and mensuration. I was only able to pick up the rudiments of these with him, but I picked them up so thoroughly that I never let them drop again.

JOSEPH ARCH

WHEN nothing out o' the way were happening, we played games in the school yard. The boys played fub-'ole with marbles and the girls played 'jinks' with five stones. Then there were round games like *There stands a lady on the mountain* and *Poor Jinny sets a-weepin'*. It seems to me now that whatever game we played used to have some sort o' words to go with it, else it weren't played right. We used to play *Fox and Hares*, a game child'en now call *Hide and Seek*. The party what were hiding went away to 'git 'id', and the other party 'ould hide their faces and chant

> When you're 'id, holler
> Else the little dugs 'on't foller.

Oranges and lemons had its own proper rhymes and so did another game we used to play called *Thread the tailor's needle*, which were a bit like oranges and lemons, the words being

> It is so dark we cannot see
> To thread the tailor's needle.

Not that we ever said it like that, because we had a family of boys from our end as coul'n't speak properly, and they used to say

> Titho dark, tannot tee
> Tithew, tathoo, nithew.

so of course we copied them. Every night there'd be two big old boys standing at the main gate o' the school yard when we come out, to dub us as we went under their arms King, Queen, 'Bacca-box, Shit-shovel, Lick-it-clean, and we used to hate it if we had to be 'Lick-it-clean'. Then there were skipping games – specially to find out who we were going to marry. You had to go and find a five-leafed clover afore you could play that game, then you could take part in *Tinker, tailor, soldier, sailor*, with all its other details.

> Coach, carriage, wheel-barrow, muck cart,
> Silk, satin, muslin, rag,
> Big 'ouse, little 'ouse, pigsty, barn.

There were rhymes for everything – some just for the saying and nothing else. We liked 'em better than the mournful poetry we were teached at school. We cupped our fists, leaving a hole between finger and thumb, and said

> Cobby's gone to market, to buy a new comb.
> Put your finger in cobby's 'ole, and see if 'e's got 'ome.

and another child would put his finger in the hole to see if it got 'squez': or we tapped our for'eads and pulled our ears and ringed our eyes with thumb and finger, lifted our noses and put a finger into our mouths as we chanted

> Knock at the door
> Ring the bell,
> Peep through the key-'ole
> Lift up the latch
> and WALK IN.

The rhymes we said were often about courting or getting married, and the ones we loved best were the vulgar ones

> Polly went a-walking one fine day
> She lost her britches by the way.
> The girls did laugh, and the boys did stare
> To see poor Polly with her backside bare.

> Clover one and clover two,
> Put it in your right foot shoe
> The first young man that you shall meet
> Shall be your sweetheart all the week.

Reply:
If his hair don't curl
And his teeth don't shine
And he ain't good looking
Then he shan't be mine.

Mary had a pudding
She made it very nice
She wouldn't stick the fork in
Till George come home at night
Georgie will you have a bit
Don't say no.

Reply:
Save it for our wedding day
Ha, ha, ho.

KATE MARY EDWARDS

43

In the very short schooling that I obtained, I learnt neither grammar nor writing. On the day that I was eight years of age, I left school, and began to work fourteen hours a day in the fields, with from forty to fifty other children of whom, even at that early age, I was the eldest. We were followed all day long by an old man carrying a long whip in his hand, which he did not forget to use.

MRS BURROWS

ELLEN BROWN, 14. – I'm in service. Went last year on the turnip land in the gangs [public]. We first cleaned the turnips, and then topped and tailed them. I got 9d. and 10d. a day. I've been out three summers and two winters. It's very cold work on the turnip land; my clothes would freeze round me. We used to go at 7 in winter and leave off at 4. I never been to school; I can't read or write.

MOTHERS of labourers' families were glad to get their girls out at an early age into any respectable family where they would be fed in return for their work.

One old woman that I knew well told me that she went out at the age of twelve.

'It was a carpenter's family,' she said, 'and there was eleven children. Yes, that was my first place, for a year. I didn't get no wages, only my food, one frock and one bonnet, and a shillin' to take home.

'Then I was hired for a year to go to a farm where the master was a widower, and after that at another farm where there was two ladies. They was the particularest ladies I ever knowd. It ud do any girl good to go and live with such as they. There was the oak stairs – it was always a clean pail of water to every two steps; and I'd as much pride in it as they had.

'My wages never got as fur as four pound. Best place I ever lived in was at Mr Woods's at Hambledon. Quietest and best master I ever lived with. There was the red-brick kitchen-floor.

I used to flow he down with a green broom; best of brooms for bricks; makes the floors red. You makes 'em of the green broom as grows on the common. After I left, there was always a bit of green holly at Christmas, and any win'fall apples he always give me. Ah! he was a good master. He minded me when I was married, and time and again he sent me a bit of beef – till he died – and then my beef died.

'One farm I lived in was nigh some rough ground where tramp people lived, and my missis use to send me out with beautiful gruel to the tramp women in the tents when there was a baby come. It was a very old farmhouse where I lived, with gurt beams athurt the ceilin'.

'But Mr Woods he was the best man. One day after I left him I was at his place, and he had a cold leg of mutton, and what does he do but take a knife and cut'n in two and give me one piece.

'And one time when bread was so dear he says, "Here's a shillin' to get a loaf" – Ah! we soon cut *he* up.

'I'm seventy-six, and some days don't know how to move about. The rheumatics they do crucify me something crool. I says if anyone wants to punish me let 'em give me a stoopin' job. It seems to turn my heart upside down.'

GERTRUDE JEKYLL

46

. . . old Biddy Wiffin has her vivid recollections too, and she has a word to say to the modern lasses. 'I can't abide all their fal-lals!' she says sometimes. I am never so indiscreet as to ask her what she means, and I assume 'fal-lals' to be some heinous vices about which it would be indelicate to inquire. Worked up to virtuous indignation she becomes voluble, and then is your time. 'Gals! there ain't no gals – they're ladies. You've got to call 'em Miss, or they'll sauce you! When I was young I *was* a gal! I was one of the lucky ones, though, I was. You mayn't credit it, but it's as true as you're sitting there: *I never had a mistress as ever give me a flogging* – not one!'

AUGUSTUS JESSOPP

47

J AMES ORTON is examined, and deposes as follows: – My name is James Orton. My father is dead; my mother lives at Wincheap. I work in the fields when I can get work. The day before yesterday I was digging; I dig from daylight till dark. I have an hour for dinner in the middle of the day. I breakfast before I start, and earn 8d. in the day. In the summer, when the wheat is up, I weed the corn; I get 6d. a-day for that. I sometimes lead the horse at plough, and get 8d. I get 6d. only for couching; it is not so hard as digging, or leading the horse at plough. I could not get any 'bird-scaring' this year; 6d. is the price of that a-day. I got 8d. at poling, for laying the poles. I picked hops; I do not know how much I got for that. I have had no digging in the hop-grounds since my father died. I cut wheat and beans this year with my mother; I do not know how much my mother got: they cut wheat and that by the acre. At beans we reap as soon as we like. It don't do to cut wheat early if there has been any damp, till eight or nine; we never begin before eight any time. If we could get two or three 'cants', we would cut beans at two in the morning, and on till dark. I have done no threshing. I have set potatoes for 8d. a-day; I have dug potatoes for 8d. a-day. I keep sheep sometimes for 6d. I don't remember what I got for clearing the ground for hops. Last summer I got 3s. 6d. a-week for keeping cows in the stables, milking, and feeding them. I have got 6d. a-day for topping and pulling up turnips. My mother has relief from the parish; I do not know how much. I have always three meals in the day: I have bread and meat for dinner, and bread and cheese for breakfast, and bread and cheese for supper. When I am not at work I do not often get bread and meat for dinner. It is ever so long since I went to school. I left off going to school before my father died, when I was about eight years old. I cannot read. I do not know the names of the months. I have good health; I have never any pains. When I do not work, I go out to play. I had rather work than play; you get most victuals when you work.

48

A little boy in this family, twelve years old, sometimes got a job to do. He got threepence a-day, and had been some days picking potatoes, where he got fourpence a-day. He sometimes drove the plough, for which he got threepence a-day. The hours at the plough were eight; but his real hours on the farm altogether being twelve each day, I mention this only to remark that the earnings of a boy at such work for such hours will not supply him with the bread he could eat. I have a lively recollection of my keen appetite when I used to be in the fields for so many hours at this age.

ALEXANDER SOMERVILLE

'I was over eighteen. I had been out in the same farmhouse three years with a man named Grimmer. He was a hoggish sort of man – what I call real hoggish – and I never liked him, and I thought I ought to get two pounds a year, and he hadn't the means. It was just the year after the war, and the farmers were breaking right and left, and I thought he'd break, and so he did; but I was beforehand with him, and I went and hired myself with a man of the name of Mills; he had that farm, you know . . . So I was to get two pounds a year, and there were five of us, men and boys, and when I got there I didn't like the looks nor the talk of the other four. When we went to bed they began to bounce a bit. "You won't be many days, young 'un," they said, "before our master will call you into his little yard." And when I asked what for, they told me that he was a rare 'un for the whip, and he gave it to them all round, young and old. We had to be down and out by five o'clock, and two or three days after I'd been there I was late. When I came down, there he was. He was a big powerful man, with wrists like a cart-horse's fore legs, but he was lamish and walked with a stick.

'"Boy," says he, "go you and fetch my whip and bring it me in the little yard." But I never stirred.

'"Do you hear?" says he, and his great voice was like a bull's.

'"I hear," says I, "but I'm not coming."

'Out he jumped, and he was that mad that he was no more lame than you are; he was as nimble as a cat. And there he'd got me griped in his left hand, and one of those brewer's whips, all one piece and six feet long, in the other. And there were those four looking on to see if I'd give in, and he took me up as if I'd been a puppy, and flung me a couple of yards off, and swish it came. I was stubborn, and that mad that I felt no more than if he'd been hitting an anvil. He certainly would have killed me if the team man hadn't called out to him, "Master, you'll be hung next assizes for killing that boy."

'Then he went in, and then I found my clothes were cut as if it had been with a knife, and I was bleeding all over. He wasn't such a bad master, though, for all that. O' course he used to flog us, but then, when he did, you see he meant it 'cause o' them wrists.'

AUGUSTUS JESSOPP

50

'OH, I've played all sorts o' games. This we used to play in a barn. We'd get hold o' one of the softies, an' make he give us he's cap. He was blindfolded. Then we called out "Pee-wit", and he had to say "More yet". Every time he said "More yet" we put some muck in his cap – ontil 't last when he come to git it, he found somethin' in it!'

I spoke of a variant of this game, going by the name of 'Church-afire'.

'A dirty game 't is,' Bettesworth repeated. 'An' then there was "Catchin' the Owl". We used to play that in a kind o' stable place. We'd go up the loft with a pail o' water, an' git the softy to stand at the bottom o' the ladder with a sieve. "Hold it up over yer head," we told 'n, so's to catch the owl when we throwed it down to 'n. Then, when he'd got it well up over his head, we soused the water down into the sieve, and 't all went through an' purty near drowned 'n . . . But the best game as ever we played – there was four or five of we boys got strings wi' crooked pins in the ends. 'Twas out' – I cannot remember where. Under trees, and in a kind of farmyard. Summer weather, I imagine – 'We put peas on the end o' these strings, and there we was, haulin' in

76

the pigeons as fast as we mind to. An' all the time, there was the bailiff down the end o' the field see all our game. He come up all of a sudden – "You damn young rascals!" and he collared hold o' me an' let me 'ave it! The others, they went for to run; but no – he caught two of 'em, an' as soon as he let go o' me I was off. I was the fust of 'em to git a threshin', but after all the others copped it worse 'n what I did . . . Oh, we did have all sorts o' games. Dirty games some of 'em was, too.'

GEORGE BOURNE

51

MARY RENDALLS, wife of Patrick Rendalls, Exeter, labourer. I was born at Shoobrook; my father was a mason. I am 41 years old. I was apprenticed between eight and nine to Mr Thomas Nicholls, farmer, of Lower Woodrow. It was a small farm. There were farm-servants kept, sometimes two men, sometimes a couple of boys; he worked himself upon the farm. I stopped with him till I was 16. He had a wife, three girls and a boy, the eldest a year older than me. Generally we had good food, better than many apprentices had, as I have heard them tell; other times not so good. For breakfast we had broth, meat boilings, sometimes made with roasting fat, sometimes with flour and butter, and bread. According to master's temper we got a piece of bread and cheese. For dinner sometimes we had peas, a basin of broth, a rasher of bacon, sometimes boiled mutton, sometimes potatoes and milk, sometimes apple-dumplings, – in such cases no meat. For supper we had a basin of broth, sometimes a fried piece of bacon and potatoes. We always had wheaten bread. When afterwards I went to service near Bridport we had nothing but barley-bread; there is nothing like wheaten bread. I always lived better than if I had been at home; I always had a bellyfull.

When I was an apprentice, I got up as early as half-past two, three, four, or five, to get cows in, feed them, milk them, and look after the pigs. I then had breakfast, and afterwards went into the fields. In the fields I used to drive the plough, pick stones, weed, pull turnips, when snow was lying about, sow corn, dig potatoes, hoe turnips, and reap. I did everything that boys did. Master made me do everything. I took a pride to it, when I used to reap, to keep up with the men.

My mistress was a very bad temper; when bad tempered she treated me very ill; she beat me very much; she would throw me on the ground, hold me by the ears, kneel upon me, and use me very ill; I used to scream. This has happened several times a-week. I have not been free from sore from one week to another. I have still marks upon me from kicks. At other times she treated me pretty well. When she was violent, we had not enough to eat.

My master beat me, and I went home to my father's house. My father was afraid to let me stop, as he might be summoned, as I was an apprentice. My brother took me to Chedworth, about 16 miles off, to prevent my going to Bridewell. I then got a place.

There were many bad places in the same parish; people used to dread the time when the children were to go out. Apprentices were often badly used at that time; not so bad now, things are more looked into.

          'I've lived i' one place all my life, Sir;
  'And, for my work, I can do all that belongs to a farm:
'I can hoe turnips and wheat; and plough (as you saw me) and
     harrow;
  'Fettle both horses and cows; clean out the stable and byre;
'Milking, of course, I can do; and poultry and pigs, and the
     dairy;
  'Reaping in harvest time; haymaking, stacking, an' all –
'And for indoors, I clean, and scrub, and attend to the
     housework;
  'Washing and ironing, too; baking and brewing, sometimes;
'Cleaning of knives and boots'

A. J. MUNBY

53

The girls go to the hirings, and like it. They wear their best
clothes, and their white veils and bonnets. They often look a
lump better than the gentry, for they look fresher like.

MRS BLACK

. . . this is the morning of stattice, and Johnny is dressed out in his best; his clean blue or white smock frock is drawn up through the openings that lead to his pockets. You see a portion of his substantial corduroys, with pearl buttons at the knees, and a length of strong drab riband; his worsted stockings, which are generally ribbed, fit as if they were glued to his legs; while his high-ancle, heavy-nailed boots glitter again with grease – you feel that you could not walk a hundred yards in them, so heavily are they shod with iron. His neckerchief is generally red, or blue, or yellow, flowered or spotted; his sleeved waistcoat a warm plush, the richest pattern he can find; his hat has the nap rubbed the wrong way down, to let you see it is 'real beaver'. He carries a stick, which he cut himself; and when he is in serious conversation, he every now and then thrusts the knob of it into his mouth. Molly mostly has a pair of pattens in the left hand, and an umbrella in the right, rarely either wearing the one or putting up the other, unless she is going home. Her gown, if in summer, is the gaudiest print that can be purchased, covered with enormous somethings between a cabbage and a dahlia. Her shawl is also of a glaring colour; and she is very fond of wearing either red or blue ribbons in her bonnet, shaped into tremendous bows. Her hands are rough as rasps, and almost as hard, through scouring kits, and other household drudgery. If she wears gloves, they make her feel uncomfortable; so much has she exposed her hands to water and weather, that they fairly burn again, and the gloves are soon thrust into her pocket. She wears a large gilt brooch, with a piece of yellow cut glass in the centre as big as the eye of an ox; but, above all, she prides herself on a smart shoe and stocking; and will sometimes, when the roads are dirty, bring a clean pair of the latter in her pocket, which she puts on in some retired corner of the fields or woods, just before entering the market-town or village. She has at times a colour like the rose, and here and there you will see a neck, that has escaped the sun, almost as white as the milk in her own dairy, while her eyes are generally of that bright, cheerful, shifting colour, called hazel, looking dark at a distance, yet as if you can see through them when near. Her lips are full, round, and open; and when her mouth is in repose, you can see the white teeth between. She is the image of embodied health, and can eat fat bacon like a ploughman; and as to work, from morning until night she does nothing but sing over it.

She meets John, with whom she had, perhaps, lived in service a year or two before, and of whom she had only heard of from a fellow-servant once or twice since that time; or she had seen him at a feast, and he regretted that he did not still live in the same place with her, and we know not what beside, though the following dialogue takes place: – John, stopping short as he sees her approach, and lifting up his stick high above his head in astonishment, exclaims, 'Lauks, Molly! sewerly it caun't be thee, neither. And how is't, my wench? – and how's all at hoam? – our old measter and missus, and all on 'em, at Grinley-on-the-Hill?'

'Why, John, this is a sirprize, for cartain,' says Molly, without answering a single question; 'an' how beest thee? an' Betty? I heard it waur to be a match. And hez to gotten hired, or hed a bidding, or only cum out for a holiday like?'

'Noah!' replies John, sucking the knob of his stick. 'I hed a bidding, but he nobert bid twelve pound, and I axed fourteen. But I'm to call on him at the Black's Head, waur he puts up, afore I goe hoam' – and here the conversation is interrupted by a farmer, whose eye having alighted upon John, he steps up and begins as follows: – 'Are you hired, my young man?'

'Noah, zur; I wishes to be, if we can come to terms.'

'What have you been used to?' inquires the farmer.

'All sorts of labouring work,' says John; 'ploughing, sowing, manuring, and helping at harvest, seeing after the cattle, and sike like.'

'Who did you live with last?' is the next question.

'Measter Duckles, of Thonock Hill Farm,' says John; 'a good measter, but rather short handed; for, beside having to do moast all the work at lambing season, I had to go to town with the team, and that was more than we bargained for'; and into his mouth went the stick, for this was a very long speech for John.

'These hard times make us clip close,' says the farmer, tapping his boot with the butt-end of his whip, and musing for a moment; then adding, 'I should, at times, require you to do the same. What wages are you asking?'

John replies; then selects a choice bit in his stick which he gnaws whilst awaiting the answer.

The farmer finds no fault with the wages, giving John to understand that there will be no abatement in the work, from what he had at the last place. Then looking at Molly, he asks John if they have lived in service together; is told when, where, and how long ago; inquires her working qualities, and receives satisfactory answers; tells John that the two servants who have lived with him for four or five years, are about to marry; and, knowing that love makes labour light, jokes John about his doing the same some day if he hires Molly; whereat John grins, and has recourse to his stick; whilst the farmer agrees with Molly; taking them both, perhaps, into the public-house, and, after fixing the day when they are to come, giving them a crown piece (if he is generous) for their fasten-penny.

THOMAS MILLER

We would stand about in groups, either in the market or the adjoining streets, until a farmer came along. After eyeing us over like so many oxen, he would say: 'Nah, my lads, any on yer seeking a place?' Being warmed up with good ale, we answered truculently, or offhandedly at least, that we didn't 'care a damn whether we got a place or not', and, 'What sort o' chap are yer wanting?'

He would then say, 'wagoner', 'seconder', 'stable-lad', or 'cow-lad', according to which he wanted, and after singling out a man or boy that took his fancy would begin questioning him on his qualifications.

'Can ta ploo, thack, stack, and drive a binder, manage three horses abreast, and carry barley?' There was no end of questioning from both sides, for the 'fastening-penny' cut both ways, and neither man nor master could part company under a twelve-month without some lawful excuse.

FRED KITCHEN

56
Country Hirings

Come all you blooming country lads and listen unto me,
And if I do but tell the truth I know you will agree.
It's of the jolly farmers who servants want to have,
For to maintain them in their pride and be to them a slave.

Servant men stand up for wages,
When to the hirings you do go,
For you must work all sorts of weather,
Both in cold, in wet, and snow.

The farmer and his wife in bed so snug and warm can lie,
While you must face the weather, both cold, wet, and dry;
For the rates they are heavy, and the taxes they are high,
And we must pull the wages down, the farmers they do cry.
Servant men stand up, etc.

The farmers twenty years ago could their rents and taxes pay,
But now they are so full of pride, it increases every day;
Which makes the landlords raise the rent, and the farmers for
    to scold,
On the poor young servant lad, and rob him of his gold.
Servant men stand up, etc.

The farmer and the servants together used to dine,
But now they're in the parlour with their pudding, beef and
    wine,
The master and the mistress, their sons and daughters all
    alone,
And they will eat the meat, and you may pick the bone.
Servant men stand up, etc.

The farmers' daughters used to dress both neat, clean and
    brown,
But now with bustles, frill and furbelows, and flounces to their
    gowns,
They do get dress'd like dandy Bess, more fitter for the stage,
Which cause the farmers' rents to rise and puts them in a rage.
Servant men stand up, etc.

The description of your living, I'm sure it is the worst,
For the pottage it is thin and the bread is very coarse,
While the masters they do live, as you shall understand
On butter and good cheese and the fat from off the land.
Servant men stand up, etc.

A roasted goose for dinner, likewise a leg of lamb,
With soups and potatoes and everything that's grand,
While the servants in the kitchen they do both sport and play,
Speaking about the fun they'll get upon the hiring day.
Servant men stand up, etc.

I could tell you of a better plan, without fear or doubt.
If you'd but kiss the mistress when the master he is out;
You may kiss her, you may squeeze her, you may roll her
    round about,
And she will find you better food, without fear or doubt.
Servant men stand up, etc.

TRADITIONAL

57

The Wheat Ripening

WHAT time the wheat field tinges rusty brown
 And barley bleaches in its mellow grey
Tis sweet some smooth mown baulk to wander down
Or cross the fields on footpaths narrow way
Just in the mealy light of waking day
As glittering dewdrops moist the maidens gown
And sparkling bounces from her nimble feet
Journeying to milking from the neighbouring town
Making life bright with song – and it is sweet
To mark the grazing herds and list the clown
Urge on his ploughing team with cheering calls
And merry shepherds whistling toils begun
And hoarse tongued bird boy whose unceasing calls
Join the larks ditty to the rising sun

JOHN CLARE

58

Bird Starver's Cry

HI! Shoo all o' the birds
 Shoo aller birds
  Shoo aller birds

Out of master's ground
Into Tom Tucker's ground

Out of Tom Tucker's ground
Into Tom Tinker's ground

Out of Tom Tinker's ground
Into Luke Collis' ground

Out of Luke Collis' ground
Into Bill Vater's ground

Hi! Shoo aller birds
Kraw! Hoop!

TRADITIONAL

59

I was a youngster of nine when I began to earn money. My
first job was crow-scaring, and for this I received fourpence
a day. This day was a twelve hours one, so it sometimes
happened that I got more than was in the bargain, and that was
a smart taste of the farmer's stick when he ran across me outside
the field I had been set to watch. I can remember how he would
come into the field suddenly, and walk quietly up behind me;
and, if he caught me idling, I used to catch it hot.

JOSEPH ARCH

As to bird-keeping, it may appear cruel that a child should have to pass some eight or ten hours a-day apart from all human society, its sole employment the frightening birds from the corn; but I have never yet had any reason to believe that the boys so employed in any way suffer injury from it. Towards the end of the day, they are, doubtless, anxious to return home, and their inquiries of passers-by as to 'what o'clock it is', prove how gladly they watch for the hour that is to release them from their day's labour; but this, after all, is no more than any schoolboy feels, who is anxious for the hour when business for the day concludes, and he is released from his books and invited to his evening meal. That these juvenile watchmen do contrive to mix up amusement with their toil, no one who has observed their labyrinths cut in turf, or their carving on gates, trees, or sticks, can doubt; for my own part, I think the importance of their trust, and the knowledge that they are earning wages, goes far to lighten the effect of the monotony of their employment.

HON. AND REV. S. GODOLPHIN OSBORNE

From the time he was nine Joseph would spend long, lonely days in school vacations and on Saturdays scaring crows off the short, green corn. He had a wooden clapper, but if he saw no one for hours he took to shouting so as to hear a human voice. This method had another convenience; you couldn't cry while you shouted.

M. K. ASHBY

The Crow Boy

WHEN I was but a baredless boy,
  Nor more'n six years owd,
I us'd t'goo a keepin' crows
  In rain an' wind an' cowd.
An' well I du remember now,
  Ah, well as it can be,
My little house, a hurdle thatch'd,
  In th' mash agin th' sea.
Car woo! car woo! yow owd black crow,
  Goo fly awa' to Sutton;
If yow stop heer't'll cost ye dear,
  I'll kill ye ded as mutton.

I used t'rise up wuth th' sun,
  'Cos crows is arly bahds;
Full oft tha've made me howl an' run
  An' sa' all kinds er wuds.
Th' moor I scar'd th' moor tha' teazed,
  An' kep' me on fer hours,
Till my poor feet, an' legs, an' knees
  Had ommost lost their pow'rs.
Car woo! car woo! etc.

An' if I tried t' git a rest,
  Th' warmen fared t'know,
Fer where at fust was on'y one
  A flock wood quickly grow.
I scream'd until my voice was hoos,
  Just like a young colt's na',

An' when it got so werry thick,
   In whispers did I say –
Car woo! car woo! etc.

But if it friz right sharp all night,
   I'd sum rest in th' morn –
Owd crows can't du no harm, ye know,
   When hud th' ground is frorn.
Yet at th' thaw tha' punish'd me;
   So when I went t'bed
I dreamt that I was in th' mash,
   An' o'er an' o'er I said,
Car woo! car woo! etc.

Th' crows at last becum so bold
   That I was well nigh dun,
Then master he took pity and
   Said yow shall have a gun.
A gun I had, an' powder tew;
   T' fire it off I tried;
Th' blam'd thing kick'd an' knock'd me down,
   But I get up an' cried,
Car woo! car woo! etc.

Now since I've grown t' be a man
   I've borne with harder blows,
An' know there's many wusser things
   Than them ere rilin' crows.
I've wish'd myself a boy agin,
   Altho' I'm gettin' gra',
An', cood it be, I'd march right off
   To that ere mash an' sa',
Car woo! car woo! etc.

TRADITIONAL

NEARLY every boy in the village carried in his pocket a catapult made from a Y-shaped peeled stick and an 18 inch length of rough rubber folded in half, the folded end being placed in a small split at the top of the Y and bound securely with twine. The other ends were fastened to a piece of pliable leather about 4 inches square. We used horse beans, small stones and even, sometimes, big shot as ammunition, and in careless hands these catapults could be very dangerous if anyone got in the way when they were being 'fired'. Children were not the only ones to make these weapons, though. Plenty of men carried them in their pockets, especially when they were out in the woods and the gamekeepers were not about, and I have known some who could cut off a pheasant's head at a distance of twenty yards. I always carry one today, but I have never been as good a shot as that, though I have hit and killed a rat from 15 yards away.

ARTHUR RANDELL

64

The Gallows

THERE was a weasel lived in the sun
   With all his family,
Till a keeper shot him with his gun
And hung him up on a tree,

Where he swings in the wind and rain,
In the sun and in the snow,
Without pleasure, without pain,
On the dead oak tree bough.

There was a crow who was no sleeper,
But a thief and a murderer
Till a very late hour; and this keeper
Made him one of the things that were,
To hang and flap in rain and wind,
In the sun and in the snow.
There are no more sins to be sinned
On the dead oak tree bough.

There was a magpie, too,
Had a long tongue and a long tail;
He could both talk and do –
But what did that avail?
He, too, flaps in the wind and rain
Alongside weasel and crow,
Without pleasure, without pain,
On the dead oak tree bough.

And many other beasts
And birds, skin, bone, and feather,
Have been taken from their feasts
And hung up there together,
To swing and have endless leisure
In the sun and in the snow,
Without pain, without pleasure,
On the dead oak tree bough.

EDWARD THOMAS

J OHN JOHNSON, a labourer, was on Wednesday committed to Peterborough, for 3 months, to atone for the offence of being taken, by one of the Marquis of Exeter's gamekeepers, with a hare in his basket. The keeper had previously traced footsteps in the snow which led to a snare, and upon watching, saw Johnson go to it on his way home, but take nothing, for the best of reasons, there was nothing to take. He, however, followed him, and found he had a hare in his possession. The culprit, if such he can be called under all the circumstances, is a hardworking labourer with a wife and two children. He walked every morning from Ketton to Southorp, and back every evening – a journey of sixteen miles: in the interim he performed a day's work: and at the end of the week he received as a reward for his labour the pittance of eight shillings. No wonder that he picked up a hare to eke out such an existence. Upon being committed he said that but for the feelings he had for his wife and children, imprisonment would be to him a luxury.

STAMFORD NEWS

66

The Sledmere Poachers

C OME, all you gallant poaching lads, and gan alang with me,
And let's away to Sledmere woods, some game for to see;
It's far and near, and what they say it's more to feel than see,
So come my gallant poaching lads, and gan alang with me.

We are all brave poaching lads, our names we dare not tell,
And if we meet the keeper, boys, we'll make his head to swell.

On the fifth of November last, it being a star-light night,
The time it was appointed, boys, that we were all to meet,
When at twelve o'clock at midnight, boys, we all did fire a gun,
And soon my lads, it's we did hear, old hares begin to run.
We are all brave poaching lads, etc.

We have a dog, they call him Sharp, he Sledmere woods did
    stray,
The keeper he fell in with him and fain would him betray;
He fired two barrels at the dog, intending him to kill,
But by his strength and speed of foot he tript across the hill.
We are all brave poaching lads, etc.

All on one side and both his thighs he wounded him full sore,
Before we reached home that night with blood was covered
    o'er;
On recovering of his strength again, revenged for evermore,
There's never a hare shall him escape that runs on Sledmere
    shore.
We are all brave poaching lads, etc.

We have a lad, they call him Jim, he's lame on all one leg,
Soon as the gun is shoulder'd up, his leg begins to wag;
When the gun presented fire, and the bird came tumbling
    down,
This lad he kick'd him with his club before he reached the
    ground.
We are all brave poaching lads, etc.

94

So as we marched up Burlington road we loaded every gun,
Saying if we meet a keeper bold we'll make him for to run,
For we are all bright Sledmere lads, our names we will not
    tell,
But if we meet a keeper bold we'll make his head to swell.
We are all brave poaching lads, etc.

We landed into Cherry woods; we went straight up the walk;
We peak'd the pheasants in the trees, so softly we did talk;
We mark'd all out, what we did see, till we return'd again,
For we were going to Colleywoodbro' to fetch away the game.
We are all brave poaching lads, etc.

Come, all you gallant poaching lads, if I must have my will,
Before we try to shoot this night lets try some hares to kill;
For shooting as you very well know, it makes terrible sound,
So if we shoot before we hunt we shall disturb the ground.
We are all brave poaching lads, etc.

We landed into Suddaby fields, to set we did begin,
Our dog he was so restless there, we scarce could keep him in;
But when our dog we did let loose, 'tis true they call him
    Watch,
And before we left that ground that night he fifteen hares did
    catch.
We are all brave poaching lads, etc.

So it's eight cock-pheasants and five hens, all these we marked
    right well.
We never fired gun that night but down a pheasant fell.
You gentlemen wanting pheasants, unto me you must apply,
Both hares and pheasants you shall have, and them right
    speedily.
We are all brave poaching lads, etc.

So now my lads, it's we'll gan yam, we'll take the nearest way,
And if we meet a keeper bold his body we will bray;
For we are all bright Sledmere lads, our names we will not
   tell,
And if we meet a keeper bold, his head we'll make to swell.
We are all brave poaching lads, etc.

So come, you poaching lads, who love to hunt the game,
And let us fix a time when we will meet again;
For at Colleywoodbro' there's plenty of game, but we'll gan
   no more.
The next port shall be Kirby Hill where hares do run by
   scores!
We are all brave poaching lads, etc.

TRADITIONAL

67

WHEN I was a lad, there used to be a gang of poachers in
our village; they went out at night as regularly in the
seasons as others went to their day's work and their harvesting.
There were, I believe, four or five, or maybe more, of them. The
gang broke up some years ago. One or two are still alive, and
following constant work; the others are old, or dead. A profes-
sional or gang-poacher generally gave it up when he was about
fifty or so, because he began then to get stiff, and lost his speed.
Poaching means very quick work, and, to succeed at it, a man is
bound to be a fast runner, agile, and quick-witted.

JOSEPH ARCH

The Poachers

WHEN I was bound apprentice in famed
     Northamptonshire,
I serv'd my master faithfully for almost seven year
Till I took up to poaching as you shall quickly hear,
Oh it's my delight on a shiny night in the season of the year.

As me and my companions were setting of a snare
The gamekeeper he was watching us, for him we did not care,
For we can wrestle and fight my boys, jump over anywhere,
For it's my delight on a shiny night in the season of the year.

As me & my companions were setting four or five,
And taking of them up again we took the hare alive,
We popped him into the bag my boys and through the wood
    did steer,
For it's my delight on a shiny night in the season of the year.

We threw him over our shoulders and wandered through the
    town,
Call'd into a neighbour's house and sold him for a crown,
We sold him for a crown my boys but did not tell you where,
For it's my delight on a shiny night in the season of the year.

Then here's success to poaching, for I do think it fair,
Good luck to every Innkeeper that wants to buy a hare,
Bad luck to every gamekeeper that would not sell his deer,
It is my delight on a shiny night in the season of the year.

TRADITIONAL

THERE was a notorious occasion at a village meeting when he clashed over some local matter with the late Alfred Turner, of Brox Hill, Oadby, a well known hosiery manufacturer and farmer. Hawker embarrassed his fellows by heatedly describing Turner to his face as 'a hard-fisted old Tory'. Turner responded by saying: 'If ever you come on my land again, I'll have you arrested for the poaching blackguard you are.'

They did not speak again for a year or more. Then one night in a thick fog, they happened to meet stepping off a tram. Turner spoke first. 'Jim,' he said, 'I think we were both fools at that meeting. Will you shake hands and be friends?'

The old poacher clutched his hand. 'Thank God, Mr Turner. Sir, this has kept me awake at night. I'm glad we can be friends again.' Slowly the couple trudged along the village street, talking amicably together. As they parted, Turner said: 'I'm pleased we're friends again. If ever you want a rabbit, I'll tell my men you can come and get it on my land any time you like.'

'Thank you kindly, Mr Turner,' replied Hawker, 'but I'm sorry you've said that. You've been honest with me, so I'll be quite frank with you. I shan't get any more of your rabbits than I've been poaching from you over this past year – only now you've given me permission it won't be half as much fun getting them.'

GARTH CHRISTIAN

I T has been the custom in our neighbourhood, ever since I was a boy, that if a woman was cleaning turnips in a field she might take two or three, once or twice in a week. Farmers did not object, as a rule, and I have often seen women when turnip-cleaning put some into their aprons before the employer's face; it was an understood thing. Farmers have made such offers of turnips to me, and of course I have taken them; I no more thought of refusing them than I would have thought of refusing to put my week's wages in my pocket. After the Act came into operation the police set upon these women – respectable, honest, married women – searched them, brought them before the magistrate at Warwick, and charged them with stealing turnips. The police prosecuted and gave evidence, and the women were fined. It was a very great shame, and the village people were very bitter and sore about it.

JOSEPH ARCH

71

The Bad Squire

T HE merry brown hares came leaping
   Over the crest of the hill,
Where the clover and corn lay sleeping
   Under the moonlight still.

Leaping late and early,
    Till under their bite and their tread
The swedes and the wheat and the barley
    Lay cankered and trampled and dead.

A poacher's widow sat sighing
    On the side of the white chalk bank,
Where under the gloomy fir-woods
    One spot in the ley throve rank.

She watched a long tuft of clover,
    Where rabbit or hare never ran;
For its black sour haulm covered over
    The blood of a murdered man.

She thought of the dark plantation,
    And the hares, and her husband's blood,
And the voice of her indignation
    Rose up to the throne of God.

'I am long past wailing and whining –
    I have wept too much in my life:
I've had twenty years of pining
    As an English labourer's wife.

'A labourer in Christian England,
    Where they cant of a Saviour's name,
And yet waste men's lives like the vermin's
    For a few more brace of game.

'There's blood on your new foreign shrubs, squire,
    There's blood on your pointer's feet;
There's blood on the game you sell, squire,
    And there's blood on the game you eat.

'You have sold the labouring-man, squire,
    Body and soul to shame,
To pay for your seat in the House, squire,
    And to pay for the feed of your game.

'You made him a poacher yourself, squire,
    When you'd give neither work nor meat,
And your barley-fed hares robbed the garden
    At our starving children's feet;

'When, packed in one reeking chamber,
    Man, maid, mother, and little ones lay;
While the rain pattered in on the rotting bride bed,
    And the walls let in the day.

'When we lay in the burning fever
    On the mud of the cold clay floor,
Till you parted us all for three months, squire,
    At the dreary workhouse-door.

'We quarrelled like brutes, and who wonders?
    What self-respect could we keep,
Worse housed than your hacks and your pointers,
    Worse fed than your hogs and your sheep!

'Our daughters with base-born babies
    Have wandered away in their shame;
If your misses had slept, squire, where they did,
    Your misses might do the same.

'Can your lady patch hearts that are breaking
    With handfuls of coals and rice,
Or by dealing out flannel and sheeting
    A little below cost price?

'You may tire of the jail and the workhouse,
    And take to allotments and schools,
But you've run up a debt that will never
    Be paid us by penny-club rules.

'In the season of shame and sadness,
    In the dark and dreary day,
When scrofula, gout, and madness
    Are eating your race away;

'When to kennels and liveried varlets
    You had cast your daughter's bread,
And, worn out with liquor and harlots,
    Your heir at your feet lies dead;

'When your youngest, the mealy-mouthed rector,
    Lets your soul rot asleep to the grave,
You will find in your God the protector
    Of the freeman you fancied your slave.'

She looked at the tuft of clover,
    And wept till her heart grew light;
And at last, when her passion was over,
    Went wandering into the night.

But the merry brown hares came leaping
    Over the uplands still,
Where the clover and corn lay sleeping
    On the side of the white chalk hill.

CHARLES KINGSLEY

So much for the Sacred Game. There is no Man in England who Run more Risks, Been in more Dangerous Scrapes than me. Yet the only time I have Been in Prison was Not for Poaching but for getting a Poor Old widow woman a Bundle of Sticks as she had no coal. A Man who still Lives told the Keepers I had a Gun. It was a Long Piece of Ash, and they knew this Oadby man had told a Lie. But they sent me to Leicester Gaol for seven Days. They just thought it was time I was there. Ever Since then I have Poached with more Bitterness against the Class. If I am able, I Will Poach Till I Die.

JAMES HAWKER

'I wish I was a gentleman,' said one boy.
'What would you do?' he was asked.
'Sit in front of the fire and eat bull's-eyes,' he replied.

RICHARD HEATH

I got to Goudhurst to breakfast, and as I heard that the Dean of Rochester was to preach a sermon in behalf of the *National Schools*, I stopped to hear him. In waiting for his reverence I went to the Methodist Meeting-house, where I found the Sunday school boys and girls assembled, to the almost filling of the place, which was about thirty feet long and eighteen wide.

The 'minister' was not come, and the schoolmaster was reading to the children out of a *tract-book*, and shaking the brimstone bag at them most furiously. This schoolmaster was a *sleek*-looking young fellow: his skin perfectly tight: well fed, I'll warrant him: and he has discovered the way of living, without work, on the labour of those that do work. There were 36 little fellows in smock-frocks, and about as many girls listening to him; and I dare say he eats as much meat as any ten of them.

WILLIAM COBBETT

75

THE Vicar had insisted on the duty of taking the Sacraments, and she began to attend the Communion Service. With her large serious thoughts she was not over-sensitive to worldly claims, nor would she blame anyone for expecting her to take a retired place, which was her own intention. But when one Sunday she found herself before the altar among a group of well-to-do folk, and the Vicar motioned imperiously to her to give way to a farmer's wife and await a later turn, her rage boiled up. She stood there before the chancel white and still for a moment and then found expression in a voice as clear as it was passionate. '"You put me aside . . ." Job says "Thou shalt not even secretly favour persons", and Paul wrote "No respect of persons with God, no distinction between Jew and Greek; the same Lord is Lord of all that call upon Him".' It was the first time that in all the centuries of Tysoe church's existence a woman's voice had been clearly raised in it to utter words of her own choosing, audible to many.

M. K. ASHBY

DURING one of my school-boy rambles I strayed into a neighbour's meadows not far from my father's house. It was in the early spring, and my object was to gather wild flowers, of which I was so very fond. I secured a tolerably large number, consisting of violets, primroses, blue-bells, and daisies, with a sprinkling of buttercups and clover. The sun was hot, and I was thirsty. Seeing a reed-covered cottage in a corner of one of the fields, I made up to the door. As I drew near I heard sounds within, as of two people conversing together. I stood on the threshold, and asked for a drink of water. Three times I asked, as the conversation seemed to go on, but no one heeded me. The door being open, I entered; and there was the good man of the dwelling quite alone in his humble room, kneeling in earnest prayer before a low form. His hands were lifted, and his face turned upwards; and so absorbed was he in his devotions, so earnestly pleading with Jehovah, that, though I repeatedly asked him for a drink of water, he never answered me, or dropped his eyes from the vision of glory which he surely beheld. I turned and left him at his devotions, bearing his image in my soul. His was true worship; and the example of this good man was not lost, I trust, upon me.

JOHN HARRIS

Afternoon Service at Mellstock

(Circa 1850)

O N afternoons of drowsy calm
    We stood in the panelled pew,
Singing one-voiced a Tate-and-Brady psalm
    To the tune of 'Cambridge New'.

  We watched the elms, we watched the rooks,
    The clouds upon the breeze,
Between the whiles of glancing at our books,
    And swaying like the trees.

  So mindless were those outpourings! –
    Though I am not aware
That I have gained by subtle thought on things
    Since we stood psalming there.

THOMAS HARDY

T HERE was one remarkable and deplorable thing about the old man, and that was his almost incredible superstition; he had sold himself to the devil, and the compact was sealed for ever and ever. It was absolutely useless to attempt to reason with him on the point, or to show the impossibility of such a thing; it had not the slightest effect, he had sold himself to 'Old Nick', and there was an end of it. How did it happen? Ah! that I could never tell. I often questioned the old man to know how the bargain was conducted, but he would never tell me that; he simply declared that he 'selled himself to Old Nick out in Maaster Pingedar's (Pinnegar's) ground, by the canal yander', when he was a young fellow. Oftentimes I tried to correct him from the error, and taught him to pray, and to think of Christ, Who came to save the world from sin, but he always burst out in piteous tears, sobbing like a child, and saying: ''Tis all right for t'other people, but nat vor I. Chent no good vor I. Old Nick got I right anough. He's allus along wi' ma, a waitin' vor ma, a swerin' and blerin' against God A'mighty; he won never let ma aloan no more.' And this delusion he continued in right up to the end, for, though many came to see him, clergy and others, and prayed no end of times, it made no difference; he was fully persuaded that he was bound to the Evil One, nothing could shake his belief in that.

ALFRED WILLIAMS

79

'ALL he kep' on about was the devil. The devil kep' comin' and botherin' of 'n. 'Tis a bad job. I s'pose he went right into it – studyin' about these here places nobody ever bin to an' come back again to tell we. Nobody don't know nothin' about it. 'Ten't as if they come back to tell ye. There's my father, what bin dead this forty year. What a crool man he must be not to 've come back in all that time, if he was able, an' tell me about it. That's what I said to Colonel Sadler. "Oh," he says, "you better talk to the Vicar." "Vicar?" I says. "He won't talk to me." Besides, what do he know about it more 'n anybody else?'

GEORGE BOURNE

Bettesworth was 'huckin' about' in his garden when the curate passed by from church.

'He stopped an' he says, "Bettesworth, I wish this 'ere Sunday work was done away with altogether." I looked at 'n an' I says, "Well, sir," I says, "if it was, I dunno what in the world'd become o' you." He went off, an' my neighbour what was standin' near by says, "You fitted 'n that time, Freddy, 'bout as tight as ever I see." Well, and I was right. He only works Sundays.'

GEORGE BOURNE

81

Farmer Dunman's Funeral

'Bury me on a Sunday,'
    He said; 'so as to see
Poor folk there. 'Tis their one day
    To spare for following me.'

With forethought of that Sunday,
    He wrote, while he was well,
On ten rum-bottles one day,
    'Drink for my funeral.'

They buried him on a Sunday,
    That folk should not be balked
His wish, as 'twas their one day:
    And forty couple walked.

They said: 'To have it Sunday
　　Was always his concern;
His meaning being that one day
　　He'd do us a good turn.

'We must, had it been Monday,
　　Have got it over soon,
But now we gain, being Sunday,
　　A jolly afternoon.'

THOMAS HARDY

82

JUST as the Magdalen Baptists had an Anniversary Sunday
every Summer the Primitive Methodists always held a
special Camp Meeting in a field where a farm wagon, sur-
rounded by seats, had already been put up. There was a lot of
hymn singing accompanied by a concertina and a fiddle and a
number of preachers – known as Ranters – from all round the
Methodist circuit would get up in turn on to the wagon and
address the huge crowd. Before the evening service began the
Methodists always paraded round the village singing at the tops
of their voices as they walked, some of them backwards, a song
which ran something like this:

I walked along the road one day,
I met a pilgrim on the way;
I said to him, 'Are you a planter?'
He said to me, 'No, I'm a ranter.'
Hallelujah! Hallelujah!

ARTHUR RANDELL

Coming through the village of Benenden, I heard a man at my right talking very loud about *houses! houses! houses!* It was a Methodist parson, in a house close by the road side. I pulled up, and stood still, in the middle of the road, but looking, in silent soberness, into the window (which was open) of the room in which the preacher was at work. I believe my stopping rather disconcerted him; for he got into shocking *repetition*. 'Do you *know*,' said he, laying great stress on the word *know*: 'do you *know*, that you have ready for you houses, houses I say; I say do you know; do you know that you have houses in the heavens not made with hands? Do you know this from *experience*? Has the blessed Jesus *told you so*?' And on he went to say that, if Jesus had told them so, they would be saved, and that if he had not, and did not, they would be damned. Some girls whom I saw in the room, plump and rosy as could be, did not seem at all daunted by these menaces; and indeed, they appeared to me to be thinking much more about getting houses for themselves *in this world first*; just to *see a little* before they entered, or endeavoured to enter, or even thought much about, those '*houses*' of which the parson was speaking: houses with pig-styes and little snug gardens attached to them, together with all the other domestic and conjugal circumstances, these girls seemed to me to be preparing themselves for. The truth is, these fellows have no power on the minds of any but the miserable.

WILLIAM COBBETT

I T was rather more than a year after this Anniversary that Joseph Arch had come to Tysoe and young Joseph Ashby had his first inkling of the relation of religious sects to the simpler, the economic aspects of life: the labourers who could and dared make claims for themselves and their children were Primitive Methodists. Perhaps that was why he went at first mostly to the 'Primitives'. Here some of his older friends of the fields and the roads were preachers and trustees. Here, too, were proofs of the power of religion, something very interesting for a boy to contemplate – men who had been drunkards and wife-beaters, brutal fellows whose lives had been changed. There was a frank, brotherly attack in the sermons on all sorts of simple evils – drink and gaming and strong language. One old brother would scold about a game of football, thinking that the old brutal sports might be coming back. Once Joseph laid up in his memory an expression of the attitude that enabled labourers to read a deep lesson of restraint to their neighbours in the higher walks. 'Men are not equal,' said the preacher, as making a quotation. 'No! but they are brothers! Our neighbours on the farms and in the great houses be lucky and selfish and proud, and they expect you and me to put up with a lot of nonsense, but they be our brothers. Bitter in our hearts we are, but we can remember it; they and we be brothers.'

M. K. ASHBY

Apology for the Poor

M<small>R</small> Editor
In this suprising stir of patrioutism and wonderful change in the ways and opinions of men when your paper is weekly loaded with the free speech[e]s of county meetings can you find room for mine? or will you hear the voice of a poor man? – I only wish to ask you a few plain questions

Amidst all this stir about taxation and tythes and agricultural distress are the poor to receive corresponding benefits   they have been told so I know but it is not the first time they have heard that and been dissapointed   when the tax was taken from leather they was told they should have shoes almost for nothing and they heard the parliment speeches of patriots as the forthcoming propechys of a political millenium but their hopes were soon frost bitten for the tax has long vanished and the price of shoes remains just were it did   nay I believe they are a trifle dearer then they was then – thats the only difference   then there was a hue and cry about taking off the duty of Sp[i]ritous liquors and the best Gin was to be little more in price then small beer   the poor man shook his head over such speeches and looking at his shoes had no faith to believe any more of these cheap wonders so he was not dissapointed in finding gin as dear as ever – for which he had little to regret for he prefered good ale to any spirits   and now the Malt and beer tax is in full cry what is the poor man to expect   it may benefit the farmers a little and the common brewers a good deal and there no doubt the matter will end   the poor man will not find the refuse of any more use to him then a dry bone to a hungry dog – excuse the simile reader for the poor have been likened unto dogs before now   and many other of these time serving hue and cries might be noticed in which the poor man was promised as much benefit as the stork was in the fable for pulling out the bone from the Wolfs throat and who got just as much at last as the stork did for his pains

some of the patriots of these meetings seem to consider the corn law as a bone sticking in the throat of the countrys distress but I am sure that the poor man will be no better off in such a matter – he will only be 'burning his fingers' and not filling his belly by harbouring any notions of benefit from that quarter for he is so many degrees lower in the Thremometer of distress that such benefits to others will not reach him and tho the Farmers should again be in their summer splendour of 'high prices' and 'better markets' as they phrase it the poor man would still be found very little above freezing point – at least I very much fear so for I speak from experience and not from hearsay and hopes as some do   some years back when grain sold at 5 and 6 guineas a quarter I can point out a many villages where the Farmers under a combination for each others inter[e]sts would give no more in winter then 10 shillings per Week   I will not say that all did so for in a many places and at that very time Farmers whose good intentions was 'to live and let live' gave from 12 to 15 shillings per week and these men would again do the same thing but they could not compel others and there it is were the poor man looses the benefit that ought to fall to him from the farmers 'better markets' and 'high prices' for corn   I hope Mr Editor that I do not offend by my plain speaking for I wish only to be satisfied about these few particulars and I am so little of a politician that I would rather keep out of the crowd then that my hobnails should trample on the gouty toes of any one   tho I cannot help thinking when I read your paper that there is a vast number of taxable advocates wearing barrack shoes or they would certainly not leave the advocates for reform to acchieve their triumphs without a struggle   I wish the good of the people may be found at the end and that in the general triumph the poor man may not be forgotten   for the poor have many oppressors and no voice to be heard above them   he is a dumb burthen in the scorn of the worlds prosperity yet in its adversity they are found ever ready to aid and assist and tho that be but as the widows mite yet his honest feelings in the cause are as worthy as the orators proudest orations   Being a poor man myself I am naturally wishing to see some one become the advocate and champion for the poor not in his speeches but his actions   for speeches are now adays nothing but words and sound   Politicians are known to be exceedingly wise as far as regards themselves and we have heard of one who tho his whole thoughts seemd constantly professing the good of his country yet he was cunning enough to keep one thought to himself in the hour of danger when he luckily hit upon the thought of standing upon his hat to keep himself from catching cold not to die for the good of the country as some others did and to be alive as he is at this moment   now if the poor mans chance at these meetings is any thing better then being a sort of foot cushion for the benefit of others I shall be exceedingly happy but as it is I much fear it as the poor mans lot seems to have been so long remembered as to be entire forgotten

> I am sir your humble Servant
> A Poor Man

> JOHN CLARE

86

A T the Huntingdon Assizes on Wednesday, Gifford White, aged 18, was indicted for sending to Isaac Ilett a letter threatening to burn him and the other farmers of Bluntisham in their beds, and also to burn their property. The prisoner pleaded Guilty. One of the female servants of the prosecutor found a sealed letter inside his farm-yard, directed 'To the

Farmers of Bluntisham, Hunts.' She took it to her master, who opened and read it; it was in these words – 'TO THE FARMERS – We are determined to set fire to the whole of this place if you don't set us to work, and burn you in your beds if there is not an alteration. What do you think the young men are to do if you don't set them to work? They must do something. The fact is, we cannot go any longer. We must commit robbery and everything that is contrary to your wish. – I am, AN ENEMY.'

Lord Abinger sentenced him to be transported beyond the seas for the remainder of his life.

NEWS OF THE WORLD

87

T HERE are very few living now who can call to mind the old agricultural riots, though Robert Brooks, who is eighty-six, can just remember them. He says the rioters used to march in a gang, blowing horns as they neared the village, and calling on the farm men to help them break up the machinery. The gangs were composed of the roughest of the farm labourers, who came strangers to the place, and demanded the surrender of the new-fashioned implements. Farmer Brooks, of Stanford-in-the-Vale, smashed his up himself, to prevent their falling into the rioters' hands; and when they came to Bury Town, the farmer there had all his machinery hauled out in a field, and shouted out, 'Ther 'em be, look! Smash 'em up, mi bwoys!' but the rioters, with a touch of good-nature, passed by his and left them intact. Such of the rioters as were apprehended were transported to the Cape of Good Hope, or Van Dieman's Land, or Gibraltar.

ALFRED WILLIAMS

The Poor Labourers

Y ou sons of old England, now list to my rhymes,
  And I'll sing unto you a short sketch of the times,
Concerning poor labourers you all must allow,
Who work all the day at the tail of the plough.
O, the poor labourers, pity poor labourers,
That are working for five or six shillings per week.

There's many poor labourers to work they will go,
Either hedging or ditching to plough or to sow,
And many poor fellows are used like a Turk,
They do not get paid for half a days work.
O, the poor labourers, etc.

And many poor labourers I'm sorry to say
Are breaking of stones for eightpence a day;
Bread and water's the fare of the poor labouring man,
While the rich they can live on the fat of the land.
O, the poor labourers, etc.

Some pity the farmers, but I tell you now,
Pity poor labourers that follow the plough,
Pity poor children half starving and then,
Divide every great farm into ten.
O, the poor labourers, etc.

There are many young fellows you'll see every day,
For snaring a hare they are banished away,
To Van Diemen's land or to some foreign shore,
And their wives and children are left to deplore.
O, the poor labourers, etc.

There's many a farmer that's making a fuss,
While the poor are starving, can scarce get a crust,
Do away with their hounds and their hunters so gay,
And give the poor labourers a little fair play.
O, the poor labourers, etc.

Fair play is a stranger these many years past,
And pity's bunged up in an old oaken cask
But the time's fast approaching, it's very near come,
When we'll have all the farmers under our thumbs.
O, the poor labourers, etc.

TRADITIONAL

89

WE are tired of landlord M.P.s and parson J.P.s. They have been crushing us ever since we left Paradise. They got us down – feet, legs, hands, arms and shoulders. Our faces were crushed into the mud. We could not see. We have now just raised our heads, but they are resting still upon our hands. Our elbows are yet in the mud, but even in this position some of us are digging at law, others studying politics, others unions, and really it seems as though we intended mastering all the metaphysical enigmas of the day.

MR SANDS

THEY had a very bad system, which I later on was instrumental in breaking up. When a father had a boy old enough to go to school, he had to go to the parson and get a ticket before the boy was allowed to enter the school; and the mother had to go to the parson's wife to get permission for the girls to enter. This was another of their numerous dodges to keep up the power of the parson. But I upset that. I had a little grandson up from Wales. I got my wife to clean his boots and trim him up nicely, and then I told her to take him to school without first obtaining a ticket. To the school she took him right away.

'Have you a ticket?' asked the schoolmaster. Said my wife, 'Oh, my husband said I was not to get one.' 'Then I cannot admit the boy,' said the schoolmaster. My wife brought the boy back and told me what the schoolmaster had said. Here was my opportunity. I knew the Act, I had read it through and through. The Act said to me, 'You must get your boy educated.' Said I to the Act, 'With the greatest of pleasure, and whatever is due and required to be paid I will pay; but to go to the parson to ask whether I may carry out the provision of the law I never, never will!' So I just told my wife to take the boy to the school again on the following Monday morning and to tell the schoolmaster that, if he refused the child admission, I would at once write to the School Authorities and ask them to summon me before the Bench at Warwick. My wife went down and told him this. 'Oh,' said he, 'that will never do. I will accept the boy on my own responsibility. He can come in now.' After that we were not troubled very much about tickets. They knew better than to fight it out. They knew they were in the wrong, that they had not half a leg to stand on; so they kept quiet. They would have dearly liked to drive me out of the parish, neck and crop.

JOSEPH ARCH

'I was too young at the time to remember,' Mark said; 'but I've often 'eard my mother tell how savage the ol' man was one day when he came home from ploughing. He was at wukk for Squire then; and him an' two others had been ploughin' with their teams somewhere on the Home Farm. Father was in one field, and the other two was across the hedge in the next. It was March – and you know how them peewits do keep on flyin' over the furrers then, whistlin' while they goo.'

Now whenever possible Mark will bring to his aid an unusual gift for miming. It is not that words fail him, but that acting would seem to be inherent in his nature. Everything he has to tell must be made as vivid as possible; and if imitation will help in any way, he never lets the opportunity slip by. A man with a game leg, or another with some peculiarity of speech; the noise of a windmill's sails, or the sound of a newly caught trout flapping against the sides of a pail – such things inevitably call for the exercise of mimicry in him. The result is as much a tribute to his powers of observation as to the liveliness of his brain. But perhaps his best imitations are of the songs of birds. No sooner, therefore, did he speak of peewits in March, tumbling like falling petals through the air, than the wintered room where we were sitting became at once transformed by the sound of their plaintive, all-but-human cry.

'Well,' he continued, 'father was drawin' his furrer, when all of a sudden Squire appeared on the scene – as if he'd popped up out of the ground. "What d'you mean," he shouted, proper angry he was, "what d'you mean whistlin' to warn your mates that you'd seen me a-comin'?" Father said he hadn't whistled nor he hadn't seen Squire a-comin': not till the moment he spoke. "Don't you stand there, lyin' to me like that," said the old man, "or I'll sack you." Yes, that's what he said; and what's more, father knew that he meant it. Squire was a Colonel in the Militia. Oh, he used to get hisself into a rare state sometimes, though he could be as nice as pie at others. Anyway, the long and the short of it was that he bullied father into sayin' he *had* whistled to warn his mates in the next field.

'Mother used to say she never did see him so savage as he was that night. He was one of the strict sort, was father; and I expect it riled him to think he'd been bullied into tellin' a lie. "I'll show 'im yet," he said; "so I will. When the sun shines both sides o' the hedges" (he meant when summer comes, of course, only that was his old-fashion way of puttin' it); "when the sun shines both sides o' the hedges," he said, "you'll see how I'll show 'im."

'And sure enough, that very summer father 'eard they were buildin' a railway down Dunmow way; so one mornin', instead of gooin' to wukk as usual, he cleared off up to the Hall. Right up to the front door he went. "Is it anything perticler?" asked the servant who answered his ring. "Yes," said father; "very perticler, tell 'im." Presently Squire came out to see what all the fuss was about. "Do you remember that time I was ploughin', back in March," said father; "and you asked me why I whistled to warn my mates that you was a-comin'? And do you remember I said I hadn't done no such thing? Nor I hadn't: it was them peewits. But you made me tell a lie. So I've come up here this mornin' to tell you what *you* did was worse'n any lie. You bullied me; but you shan't bully me no more. I'm gooin' to wukk on the railway. Good mornin', Squire!"'

C. HENRY WARREN

'Now this 'ere Insurince Bill, sir – I s'pose you understands just all about it. Now me and Jack 'ere we can't make 'ead nor tail on it; so we agrees we'll do what other folk does, don't us, Jack?' 'Ay, ay,' replied Jack Woodward; 'in the way 'o votin' like, I jus' follows the rest on 'em. I s'pose it's about the same party as passed them ol' age penshins, isn't it, sir?' – 'Ay, ay, I thought so: then I reckon them's the chaps to vote for; but the Squire, 'e goes t'other way like, and 'e ought to know.'

CHRISTOPHER HOLDENBY

93

THIS great squire – he was a very rich, influential man – sent for me to go down to his house when my work was over, in order to canvass me. I went down, and after some talk he said to me, 'Do your Liberals find you employment?' 'What has that to do with my vote?' I said. 'I sell you my labour, but not my conscience; that's not for sale.'

'Oh!' said this big, strapping, six-foot man.

'Now look here, sir,' I said; 'I sat second horse behind you for several years, and I have worked in your stables, but since I have been out of your stables have you ever given me a sovereign without my having given you a sovereign's worth of good labour? No! You know I have always given you a sovereign's worth of labour for every sovereign you have given me, and therefore why should I give you my vote because I sell you my labour?'

'Then,' said he, 'Sit down, Joe, and have a glass of sherry.'

JOSEPH ARCH

'I be eighty come Michaelmas,' he said, 'and have lived thirty or forty years in this place; I was bred at Honeybourn, in Gloucester, and am the last of my family.'

He was deeply and truly pious; but his experience was somewhat like that of the patriarch Jacob. In answer to a question as to whether he had had much trouble:—

'No man more,' he replied. 'It's a wurruld of trouble, and I shall be glad to be out of it.'

He had had several children, but did not appear to regret it, or to think that that fact had increased his misery. A sick wife had been his life-long affliction; the poor old body lay above sixteen months bedridden.

Withal he was no grumbler, but disposed to think he had all that he was entitled to. 'Yes,' said he, 'I liked to go to church as long as I could; I was bred up to church. Our parson be very kind; he comes to see me often, and does good to body as well as soul.' Referring to the Labourers' Union he said, 'I don't think much o' this 'ere Union, and I'll tell yer why, sir. Here have I served one man or his father this forty year, and never had a misword. All the work I have done he's paid me for. How do you think, sir, such a maayster 'ud like it if I was to fly in his face and ask him for more wages? We must all do our duty, sir. The maaysters must do their duty to the men, and the men must do their duty to their maaysters'; and suddenly waxing warm, the old man exclaimed, 'England expects every man to do his duty, sir, as Lord Nelson said.'

RICHARD HEATH

THE day was February 7th, 1872. It was a very wet morning, and I was busy at home on a carpentering job; I was making a box. My wife came in to me and said, 'Joe, here's three men come to see you. What for, I don't know.' But I knew fast enough. In walked the three; they turned out to be labourers from over Wellesbourne way. I stopped work, and we had a talk. They said they had come to ask me to hold a meeting at Wellesbourne that evening. They wanted to get the men together, and start a Union directly. I told them that, if they did form a Union, they would have to fight hard for it, and they would have to suffer a great deal; both they and their families. They said the labourers were prepared both to fight and suffer. Things could not be worse; wages were so low, and provisions were so dear, that nothing but downright starvation lay before them unless the farmers could be made to raise their wages. Asking was of no use; it was nothing but waste of breath; so they must join together and strike, and hold out till the employers gave in. When I saw that the men were in dead earnest, and had counted the cost and were determined to stand shoulder to shoulder till they could squeeze a living wage out of their employers, and that they were the spokesmen of others like-minded with themselves, I said I would address the meeting that evening at 7 o'clock. I told them that I had left nine shillings a week behind me years ago, and as I had got out of the ditch myself, I was ready and willing to help them out too. I said, 'If you are ready to combine, I will run all risk and come over and help you.'

*

. . . When I reached Wellesbourne, lo, and behold, it was as lively as a swarm of bees in June. We settled that I should address the meeting under the old chestnut tree; and I expected to find some thirty or forty of the principal men there. What then was my surprise to see not a few tens but many hundreds of labourers assembled; there were nearly two thousand of them. The news that I was going to speak that night had been spread about; and so the men had come in from all the villages round within a radius of ten miles. Not a circular had been sent out nor a handbill printed, but from cottage to cottage, and from farm to farm, the word had been passed on; and here were the labourers gathered together in their hundreds. Wellesbourne village was there, every man in it; and they had come from Moreton and Locksley and Charlecote and Hampton Lucy, and from Barford, to hear what I had to say to them. By this time the night had fallen pitch dark; but the men got bean poles and hung lanterns on them, and we could see well enough. It was an extraordinary sight, and I shall never forget it, not to my dying day. I mounted an old pig-stool, and in the flickering light of the lanterns I saw the earnest upturned faces of these poor brothers of mine – faces gaunt with hunger and pinched with want – all looking towards me and ready to listen to the words, that would fall from my lips. These white slaves of England stood there with the darkness all about them, like the Children of Israel waiting for some one to lead them out of the land of Egypt.

JOSEPH ARCH

THE picture he drew of a comfortable cottage life as it should be, was so cosy, so well within the grasp of his listeners' imagination, that an old labourer in the crowd held up a coin between his finger and thumb exclaiming, 'Here's zixpence towards that, please God!' 'Towards what?' said a bystander. 'Faith, I don't know that I can spak the name o't, but I know 'tis a good thing,' he replied.

THOMAS HARDY

97

The Fine Old English Labourer

COME, lads, and listen to my song, a song of honest toil,
'Tis of the English labourer, the tiller of the soil;
I'll tell you how he used to fare, and all the ills he bore,
Till he stood up in his manhood, resolved to bear no more.
This fine old English labourer, one of the present time.

He used to take whatever wage the farmer chose to pay,
And work as hard as any horse for eighteenpence a day;
Or if he grumbled at the nine, and dared to ask for ten,
The angry farmer cursed and swore, and sacked him there and
    then.
This fine old English labourer, one of the present time.

He used to tramp off to his work while town folk were abed,
With nothing in his belly but a slice or two of bread;
He dined upon potatoes, and he never dreamed of meat,
Except a lump of bacon fat sometimes by way of treat.
This fine old English labourer, one of the present time.

He used to find it hard enough to give his children food,
But sent them to the village school as often as he could;
But though he knew that school was good, they must have
    bread and clothes,
So he had to send them to the fields to scare away the crows.
This fine old English labourer, one of the present time.

He used to walk along the fields and see his landlord's game
Devour his master's growing crops, and think it was a shame;
But if the keeper found on him a rabbit or a wire,
He got it hot when brought before the parson and the squire.
This fine old English labourer, one of the present time.

But now he's wide awake enough and doing all he can
At last, for honest labour's rights, he's fighting like a man;
Since squires and landlords will not help, to help himself he'll
    try,
And if he does not get fair wage, he'll know the reason why.
This fine old English labourer, one of the present time.

They used to treat him as they liked in the evil days of old,
They thought there was no power on earth to beat the power of
    gold;
They used to threaten what they'd do whenever work was
    slack,
But now he laughs their threats to scorn with the Union at his
    back.
This fine old English labourer, one of the present time.

TRADITIONAL

Last winter, when I have gone home at night, it has generally been as soon as I got in at the door, 'What is Robert crying for?' 'Cos there's only bread alone for supper,' was the answer. That wasn't my fort; for I didn't carry my money to the alehouse, or smoke it away in tobacco. Next night it would be just the same. Flour was 2s. 3d. a stone. Before we could eat it, it was 2s. 5d. My wages were 11s. a week. We ate 4 stones of flour a week. Reckon that up and you will see I didn't waste my money . . . I ha' to go so much a' trust, and spend my harvest money to make up arrears. I want such wages as when harvest time come I hain't to say, 'There's ten shillings for that; two pun ten for the shummaker's bill; and five shillings for another amount. I don't want to strike. I want my master to pay me so that I can live well, and maintain my family and pay as I go along. If the women had said years ago they wouldn't go for so much pen and ink (credit) then men would have then I believe have demanded more wages . . . A good missus is a good thing on a farm. If you look into my basket of an evening instead of finding a swede turnip for supper, you'd see some taters which the master or missus gave me, and a piece of mate or else bread. They are good things for my children . . . If they paid us well, they wouldn't ha' to come up to us during the day and say, 'There's very little work done.' What's the reason? Very often because a poor man's belly is empty. They say sometimes during harvest or haysel, 'So and So is knocked up and gone home. He's good for nothing.' What's the reason? 'Cos the master is putting money into his pocket that should ha' put food into our bellies . . . They say when we send our children to work that they are small and not worth their money. Whose faut is that? 'Tain't mine.

WYMONDHAM LABOURER

'How much *do* you earn?'
'I earns a smart lot more than I gets.'

HARRY FINCH

100

Aᴛ Ascot, in Oxfordshire, some men were locked out. At this
time there were small strikes going on here and there in the
county. Some Union men working for a farmer or two would ask
for Union wages. They would give notice on the Saturday that
they wanted the rise the next week. If the farmers held out and
refused it, the men would leave on the following Saturday.
There was a small local strike on at Ascot, and the carter of a
farmer there, named Hambridge, joined the strike without
giving the usual notice. Hambridge summoned him and got the
costs. Then Hambridge called in outside labour, got over, I
think it was, two men, from a village in the neighbourhood. Of
course this made the bad feeling ten times worse; it was not
dropping oil on troubled waters anyway. These Ascot women,
who had husbands out of work, thought they would drive the
men away when they came. It was but natural that they should
object to outsiders slipping into their husbands' shoes, and they
wanted to show the farmers that Ascot folk, women though they
might be, were not going to stand by and see their bread and
butter pass to strangers without some sort of protest. So when
the men came in, out marched the women and mobbed them.
The women dared them to enter Hambridge's field. The only
blows that they struck were tongue blows, though I heard that
some of them carried sticks. Hambridge took the matter up, and

the women, seventeen of them, were summoned before the magistrates at Chipping Norton.

The presiding magistrates were two clergymen – squarsons, as they called them. In their evidence the labourers, who were strapping men and not likely to be frightened and hurt by a parcel of women, gave evidence that, so far from being set upon with sticks, they had been invited by the women to come back to the village and have a drink. In fact it was plain enough to any unprejudiced person that no physical injury was attempted; at the most there might have been a little hustling, but these stalwart labourers after saying 'No, thank you,' to the offer of a drink – it was the poor women's tempting bait – went to work on Hambridge's farm under the protection of a police constable.

Of course the women pleaded 'Not guilty', and the reverend magistrates retired to consider and consult. They were a very long time about it. Then they came back into Court and passed sentence on sixteen of the women; seven were to be imprisoned with ten days' hard labour, and nine were to have seven days' hard labour. Here was a sentence to be passed by clergymen of the Church of England, on respectable working women, some of whom had children at the breast!

JOSEPH ARCH

Of course all this disputing and contending with the high and mighty ones helped to spread my name abroad, and there was not a parson or a squire in the countryside who loved the sound of it. If they could have stuck a gag in my mouth, gagged I should have been in a jiffy. If they could have clapped a muzzle on me, muzzled I should have been before I could say 'Jack Robinson!' But they could neither gag nor muzzle me. They gave me the bad name, but they couldn't hang me. They, and others of the same kidney, wrote me down a contentious brawler, a dissenting wind-bag, and a Radical revolutionary; but not one of them could say I was an idler who neglected his family, and left them to shift for themselves. The fact of my being a steady, industrious, and capable workman was a stumper for them; they could not get over that.

JOSEPH ARCH

I went over to the stone she had pointed to and read the inscription to John Toomer and his wife Rebecca. She died first, in March, 1877, aged 72; he in July the same year, aged 75.

'You knew them, I suppose?'

'Yes, they belonged here, both of them.'

'Tell me about them.'

'There's nothing to tell: he was only a labourer and worked on the same farm all his life.'

'Who put a stone over them – their children?'

'No, they're all poor and live away. I think it was a lady who lived here; she'd been good to them, and she came and stood here when they put old John in the ground.'

'But I want to hear more.'

'There's no more, I've said; he was a labourer, and after she died he died.'

'Yes? go on.'

'How can I go on? There's no more. I knew them so well; they lived in the little, thatched cottage over there, where the Millards live now.'

'Did they fall ill at the same time?'

'Oh, no, he was as well as could be, still at work, till she died, then he went on in a strange way. He would come in of an evening and call his wife. "Mother! Mother, where are you?" you'd hear him call, "Mother, be you upstairs? Mother, ain't you coming down for a bit of bread and cheese before you go to bed?" And then in a little while he just died.'

'And you said there was nothing to tell!'

'No, there wasn't anything. He was just one of us, a labourer on the farm.'

W. H. HUDSON

JOHN MAKEPEACE, the shepherd, was nearing sixty-five and looked older. He was shrivelled and bent and dirty, for he lived alone in an old, low-roofed cottage on the edge of one of Mr Ainge's two farmyards. Here he used only one room, cooked his meals on a fire of sticks in a little three-legged cauldron; his smocks he washed once a year, so it was said, in the nearest brook. He had no right to his name, someone told Joseph. An ancestor of his had been born in a ditch, of a wayfaring woman, who had died before the babe was heard crying and taken to the nearest farm. There he grew up in kitchen and stables and became Makepeaces' John, and now his descendant was John Makepeace. Living between Whatcote and Tysoe, he seldom visited either. He had never taken a near view of Compton Wynyates though it was just over the hill. It was half a century since he had entered a church – and this in 1870, when Sabbath keeping was universal. A pagan was Makepeace. Absorbed in the fields, in the animal life and in the murky jobs in his cottage, there was no room in his life for ideal or abstraction. Yet he had his comments on such matters. Periodically the Vicar hunted him down and told him he had a soul to save. 'If I never gus to church I never gus to chapel', was his ritual reply, as if that at least should please the parson.

M. K. ASHBY

Once I was a shepherd boy

Once I was a shepherd boy,
  Kept sheep on Compton Down,
'Twas about two miles from Illesley,
It was called a market town.
With my fol de rol,
O the riddle oddy O,
With my fol de rol I day.

And in the morn when we do rise
When daylight do appear
Our breakfast we do get,
To our fold we all do steer.
With my fol de rol, etc.

And when we gets to our sheepfold
We merrily pitched him round
And all the rest part of the day
We sailed the downs all round.
With my fol de rol, etc.

When we gets up on the down
Gazing ourselves all round,
We see the storm is rising
And coming on all round.
With my fol de rol, etc.

And the storm is coming on,
The rain fast down do fall,
Neither limb nor tree to shelter me,
I must stand and take it all.
With my fol de rol, etc.

And there we stood in our wet clothes,
A-shining and shaking with cold.
We dare not go to shift ourselves
Till we drive our sheep to fold.
With my fol de rol, etc.

And when the storm is over
And that you may plainly see,
I'll never keep sheep on the downs any more,
For there's neither a limb nor a tree.
With my fol de rol, etc.

TRADITIONAL

105

GABRIEL OAK had ceased to feed the Weatherbury flock for about four-and-twenty hours, when on Sunday afternoon the elderly gentlemen Joseph Poorgrass, Matthew Moon, Fray, and half-a-dozen others, came running up to the house of the mistress of the Upper Farm.

'Whatever *is* the matter, men?' she said, meeting them at the door just as she was coming out on her way to church, and ceasing in a moment from the close compression of her two red lips, with which she had accompanied the exertion of pulling on a tight glove.

'Sixty!' said Joseph Poorgrass.

'Seventy!' said Moon.

'Fifty-nine!' said Susan Tall's husband.

'– Sheep have broke fence,' said Fray.

'– And got into a field of young clover,' said Tall.

'– Young clover!' said Moon.

'– Clover!' said Joseph Poorgrass.

'And they be getting blasted,' said Henery Fray.

'That they be,' said Joseph.

'And they will all die as dead as nits, if they bain't got out and cured!' said Tall.

Joseph's countenance was drawn into lines and puckers by his concern. Fray's forehead was wrinkled both perpendicularly and crosswise, after the pattern of a portcullis, expressive of a double despair. Laban Tall's lips were thin, and his face was rigid. Matthew's jaws sank, and his eyes turned whichever way the strongest muscle happened to pull them.

'Yes,' said Joseph, 'and I was sitting at home looking for Ephesians, and says I to myself, "'Tis nothing but Corinthians and Thessalonians in this danged Testament," when who should come in but Henery there: "Joseph," he said, "the sheep have blasted theirselves –"'

THOMAS HARDY

THE shepherds idle hours are over now
      Nor longer leaves him neath the hedgrow bough
On shadow pillowd banks and lolling stile
Wilds looses now their summer friends awhile
Shrill whistles barking dogs and chiding scold
Drive bleating sheep each morn from fallow fold
To wash pits where the willow shadows lean
Dashing them in their fold staind coats to clean
Then turnd on sunning sward to dry agen
They drove them homeward to the clipping pen
In hurdles pent where elm or sycamore
Shut out the sun – or in some threshing floor
There they wi scraps of songs and laugh and tale
Lighten their anual toils while merry ale
Goes round and gladdens old mens hearts to praise
The thread bare customs of old farmers days

JOHN CLARE

107
Sheep-shearing Song

COME all my jolly boys and we'll together go,
      Together with our masters to shear the lambs and
'yowes'.
All in the month of June of all times in the year
It always comes in season the lambs and 'yowes' to shear.
And then we will work hard, my boys, until our backs do break,
Our Master he will bring us beer whenever we do lack.

Our Master he comes round to see our work's done well,
And he says, Shear them close, my boys, for there is but little
    wool,
O, yes, good Master, we reply, we'll do well as we can.
Our Captain cries, Shear close, my lads, to each and every
    man,
And at some places still we have this story all day long,
Bend your backs and shear them well, and this is all their song.

And then our noble Captain doth to the Master say,
Come let us have one bucket of your good ale, I pray,
He turns unto our Captain and makes him this reply,
You shall have the best of beer, I promise, presently.
Then with the foaming bucket pretty Betsy she doth come
And Master says, Maid, mind and see that every man has
    some.

This is some of our pastime while we the sheep do shear,
And though we are such merry boys, we work hard, I declare,
And when 'tis night and we are done our Master is more free
And stores us well with good strong beer and pipes of tobaccee,
And there we sit a-drinking we smoke and sing and roar,
Till we become far merrier than e'er we were before.

When all our work is done and all the sheep are shorn
Then home with our Captain to drink the ale that's strong.
It's a barrel then of hum-cap which we will call Black Ram,
And we do sit and swagger and we swear that we are men.
And yet before the night is through I'll bet you half-a-crown,
That if you ha'n't a special care that Ram will knock you
    down.

TRADITIONAL

At night they would fold as many of the sheep as they could in the barn under cover so that they could make a good start in the morning, because you cannot shear wet wool, whether it is wet with rain or dew. As soon as the first glimmer of the day appeared in the sky the ewes began to stir and miss their lambs and would start bleating for their absent offspring. That was the crew's alarm clock and was usually at about 4 a.m. 'C'mon then. They be ready for ye,' Uncle Tom would shout and the men would stir themselves, put on their boots and with a certain amount of grumbling, yawning and stretching, they would have a quick sloosh in a horse trough or any other water that was available and 'leather right into it'.

They were a rough and ready gang of chaps but their general standards of personal cleanliness were, for that day and age, very good. There were, of course, notable exceptions and these were not very highly thought of by their workmates. The talk turned this way one night many years later down at the Abergavenny Arms at Rodmell. We were sitting on a form at the trestle table in the crowded long room and there were several old sheep-shearers in the company. Jim and his old pal Shad, Peter Dudeney, Jack Goddens and others. They were all in their seventies by then, slower, greyer, balder and more lined about the face, of course, than they had been when they all worked together, but still singing, laughing and talking about the old days. Under the low ceiling the atmosphere was hot and smoky and the scrubbed-top table was networked with a complicated sort of Olympic Games motif in wet beer rings.

'Ol' Charlie Putten up Kingston, now, 'e wuz a dirty ol' sod if y' like. Why 'e 'adn't washed 'is fit [feet] fer thirty years.'

'A-ah! But 'e used t' walk through the pond with 'is boots on sometimes though. Specially if we 'ad a 'ot summer.'

'Yeah. 'Twere a real shame 'e 'ad to wash one an 'em in the end.'

'Oh, 'ow wuz that then?'

'Wal, an ol' cart-'orse stepped back on 'im and broke two or three of 'is toes and 'e 'ad to clean 'er up a bit afore 'e went to the doctor's.'

But to get back to sheep-shearing: the captain and lieutenant would take up their positions, one on each side of the barn door, so that while they were doing their own shearing, they could cast an eye on every sheep that was shorn as it left the barn to see if the job was up to standard. Then it would not be long before the first fleeceless victims, voicing their protest and bewilderment in a number of different keys, would emerge into the grey light of early morning looking slightly absurd and as naked as freshly peeled oranges.

The crew would stop every two hours or so to sharpen their shears, light their pipes and sit down for a pot of beer. At dinner time they had an hour in which to eat their main meal and they sometimes played a game to determine who should be the next man to get up and draw the beer from the barrel and pass it round to the rest. They sat round cross-legged and tailor fashion on the floor in a rough circle and presently one of them would start the game by throwing his legs back over his head until the toe-caps of his boots touched the floor behind him, and at the same time chanting the first line of the verse below. Then the man on his left would do likewise and call the second line and so on until the man who chanted the fourth line had to get up, go to the barrel in the corner and replenish the empty pots.

'Here goes old Adamses Bells,
Here goes old Tymothy Tuff,
O, can you see my arse,
O, yes, quite plain enough.'

BOB COPPER

Thus will the old man ancient ways bewail
    Till toiling sheers gain ground upon the tale
And brakes it off – when from the timid sheep
The fleece is shorn and wi a fearfull leap
He starts – while wi a pressing hand
His sides are printed by the tarry brand
Shaking his naked skin wi wondering joys
And fresh ones are tugd in by sturdy boys
Who when theyre thrown down neath the sheering swain
Will wipe his brow and start his tale again

JOHN CLARE

110

Sheep-shearing Song

Here's the rosebud in June, the sweet violets in bloom,
    And the birds singing gaily on ev'ry green bough,
The pink and the lily and the daffy-down-dilly,
To adorn and perfume the sweet meadows in June,
Whilst out the plough, the fat oxen go slow,
And the lads and the lassies a-sheep-shearing go.

Here's the cleanly milk pail is full of brown ale,
Our table, our table, our table we'll spread,
We will sit and we'll drink, we'll laugh, joke and sing,
Each lad takes his lass out on the green grass,
Whilst out the plough, etc.

Now the shepherds have sheared all their jolly, jolly sheep,
What joy can be greater than to talk of the increase,
Here's the ewes and the lambs, the hogs and the rams,
The fat wethers too, they'll make a fine show,
Whilst out the plough, etc.

III

AFTER the general shearing still remain
  The tenderer milch-yoes to be clipped.
A separate job, some later week,
When temperate days will hold,
– For eild sheep, wethers, hoggs, and barren yoes
Risk with less danger the returning cold.
Then may the lambs be dipped,
The lambs that frantic for their mothers seek
Who gaunt, ungainly, queer, regain the fold.
And general dipping next in order goes,
Snatched between hay and harvest, as may be,
And as the ripening and the weather fit.
This is a feast that makes the whole farm shout
With laughter as on holiday, to see
The bothered and unwilling beasts submit
And swim the tank, and scramble dripping out
With never a maggot left, or louse, or flea.
Sheep do the work, while men stand grinning by,
Knowing that work in earnest waits them after
This interlude, this funning, and this laughter,
Work in the fields, with aching thews, and sweat,
And blessed coolth only when sun has set.

VITA SACKVILLE-WEST

To-day the heat was excessive and as I sat reading under the lime I pitied the poor haymakers toiling in the burning Common where it seemed to be raining fire.

FRANCIS KILVERT

I used to turn out quite early in the morning when cutting grass, as the machine cuts better while the dew is on, besides being easier for the horses before the sun gets powerful. Several mornings I reached the field as the church clock was striking five, and I know of no pleasanter occupation than to be mowing grass at that hour, when the sun is scarcely touching the dew-drops, and not a soul about; with a stray partridge calling up its chicks, and a blackie piping atop of the ash-tree. Maybe a magpie will come scolding, for he thinks it an offence for these humans to come disturbing him before it is well daylight. Then, it seems, you see the earth as God made it.

There is something fascinating, almost evil, about the grass-reaper; unlike the binder that waits for the corn to die and then reaps, it cuts through life, sweeping down the slender moon-pennies and toppling them over into long lines of swathes. It chatters its way through tangles of wild vetches, desecrating beds of royal purple, and leaves behind it long lines of trembling grass, cocksfoot, and white clover. By seven o'clock the sun gets higher and all the grasses shimmer in drops of crystal, and the skylark dries his dewy wings in the sun, and in the shady wood the pigeons croon a drowsy note, and all the air is full of scents and hazy mists and humming bees. Another scorching day is here. Then you look at your work, and say, 'It is enough,' and go home to breakfast.

So I reaped in the early morning, and after breakfast hoed turnips, or turned the hay I had reaped the day before; and when the hay was ready, built it into neat stacks, working until nine at night, and finding days all too short because life was good.

FRED KITCHEN

114

In the haytime, Joseph was up sometimes at half-past-three in the morning, and out in the fields with the men half a mile away by four. The mowers worked six or nine in a row, each cutting a swath behind another. Their scythes went singing through the grass, and the triumph of the scythe and the rhythmic fall of the swath continued like a long, slow, sacred dance.

M. K. ASHBY

SEASON after season a farmer in this village had been very unlucky with his crops. He cut his grass at the usual time, and one day the sun dried it, and another day the rain came and wet it. So he thought the best thing would be to take the grass into the barn as soon as it was cut, and then bring the sunshine into the barn. So one day they found him busy with his cart. First he took the cart out into the sunshine, and let the sun shine on it for a few minutes, and then he began to tie the sunshine on with ropes. After he had done this he led the horses and cart into the barn, took the rope off the cart, and kicked the sunshine on to the grass.

S. O. ADDY

116

FOR the haymaking a queer old couple named Beer were engaged, not for the day, week, or season, but permanently. On some fine summer morning, without previous notice, Beer would come with his scythe to the back door and say: 'Tell Mis'is that grass be in fine fettle now an' th' weather don't look too unkind like; and with her permission I be now about to begin on't.' When he had the grass lying in swathes, his wife appeared, and together they raked and turned and tossed and tedded, refreshed at short intervals by jugs of beer or tea provided by Miss Lane and carried to them by Zillah.

Beer was a typical old countryman, ruddy and wizened, with very bright eyes; shrivelled and thin of figure and sagging at the knees, but still sprightly. His wife was also ruddy of face, but her figure was as round as a barrel. Instead of the usual sun bonnet, she wore for the haymaking a white muslin frilled cap tied under the chin, and over it a broad-brimmed black straw hat, which made her look like an old-fashioned Welsh-woman. She was a merry old soul with a fat, chuckling laugh, and when she laughed her face wrinkled up until her eyes disappeared. She was much in request as a midwife.

When the hay was dried and in cocks, Beer came to the door again: 'Ma'am, ma'am!' he would call. 'We be ready.' That was the signal for the smiths to turn out and build the hayrick, with Peggy herself and her spring-cart to do the carrying. All that day there was much running to and fro and shouting and merriment. Indoors, the kitchen table was laid with pies and tarts and custards and, in the place of honour at the head of the table, the dish of the evening, a stuffed collar chine of bacon. When the company assembled, large, foaming jugs of beer would be drawn for the men and for those of the women who preferred it. A jug of home-made lemonade with a sprig of borage floating at the top circulated at the upper end of the table.

FLORA THOMPSON

117

ONE sermon so much impressed Kathleen that her father bade her write it out – old Job's sermon on grass. Job was one of the few labouring members of the Wesleyan community, a great-grandson of one of the founders of the chapel. He was a shepherd and no appearance could have been more suitable than his for his office. He was of the long type – tall, with long face, long hands. His old clothes hung loosely about him. His face had the look of one who sympathizes and weighs, and the quickly shifting expression of almost excessive sensitiveness. Among the spruce tradesmen and well-clad young farmers his looks had become remarkable.

'It is harvest time, but I won't talk to you about harvest . . . I'm going to talk about grass. Here's my text: just "The grass of the field". You know how the full text goes. God cared for the grass so as to clothe it wi' beauty and adorn it wi' flowers.

'The pity of it is that the Bible wasn't written in a beautiful grassy country, not as I gather. Perhaps it wouldn't ha' done for Christ to walk too often up our hills in Spring. He'd not perhaps ha' thought we needed his salvation and we'd have had maybe only a Nature worship, and that for such as us is not enough. But it does me good to think of Him looking down on our ground. Beauty he loved, an' I don't doubt it lightened his suffering. There's no daisies, nor yet celandines in the Bible, not even in the Psalms. And yet it's a sight most freshening to the mind in Spring to look down the fields in this and Oxhill parish and see the daisies on the crowns of the old broad plough ridges and the celandines in the hollows between 'em. They wouldn't be there if we was to drain better, but out of ruinous farming comes the shining gold of celandines. But that's going back to the Spring of the year, which with Autumn on us, I shouldn't. Only I love to compare the seasons. The softness of this September mixes well in the mind with the blustering winds of March. And the smell of the walnut hoods challenges a body, can he remember the smell of the may and the lilac? But I am forgetting. I'm talking o' grass. Of all the natural gifts of God I thought of grass to talk about. Grass is always with us. It never fails, even in the farming sense. It clothes the whole world as with a cloak. It feeds the beasts and they feed us. Permanent grass is a rest for the thoughts. "I lay me down in green pastures." The green colour o' grass rests the eye, the neverfailingness of it rests the anxious mind; and the feel of it is rest for the body in summer season.

'The Bible says of the Spring grass "The tender grass

showeth itself." Tender – that is the word. Tender green to the eye, tender to the jaws of the young calves just turned out. The tender grass. There's one text that dooant seem to spake well o' grass. "The grass withereth." If everything withered as sweet as grass, 'twould be a good world. The grass that withers standing makes a fine music in the wind, though it takes a fine ear to hear it. And have y'ever sin the red sunset reflected on a million shinin' dry bents in autumn? It's a sight I can't talk about: but you may look for it in August when the sun's rays come level wi' the ground, out of a red sunset. I mind I see it every night o' that week when my bwoy came back from the war, back home to die. A man's eyes and ears be sharp when his blessings be slipping away.

'Ay, but that reminds me, grass robs death of its terrors, for who but feels soothed at the thought of the green grass waving over a body that is weary and hurt, and laden with hard and painful memories? When I was young my thoughts would be too much for me and I'd long to be beneath the daisies; not up in heaven. For that you want newness of spirit. But God in his mercy lets us throw off our weariness and leave it kindly buried beneath the grinsw'd.

'What I really want to say is – look around you at the common mercies of the Lord. There's trees; there's bread: and I'm saving up a sermon for you about little childer – all things that be around us now and always.

> Count your blessings,
> Name them one by one,
> And it will surprise you
> What the Lord hath done.'

M. K. ASHBY

Hᴇ was a curious-looking old man, in old frayed clothes, broken boots, and a cap too small for him. He had short legs, broad chest, and long arms, and a very big head, long and horselike, with a large shapeless nose and grizzled beard and moustache. His ears, too, were enormous, and stood out from the head like the handles of a rudely shaped terracotta vase or jar. The colour of his face, the ears included, suggested burnt clay. But though Nature had made him ugly, he had an agreeable expression, a sweet benign look in his large dark eyes, which attracted me, and I stayed to talk with him.

*

. . . He said that he was over seventy, and had spent the whole of his life in the neighbourhood, mostly with cows, and had never been more than a dozen miles from the spot where we were standing. At intervals while we talked he paused to utter one of his long shouts, to which the cows paid no attention. At length one of the beasts raised her head and had a long look, then slowly crossed the field to us, the others following at some distance. They were short-horns, all but the leader, a beautiful young Devon, of a uniform glossy red; but the silky hair on the distended udder was of an intense chestnut, and all the parts that were not clothed, were red too – the teats, the skin round the eyes, the moist embossed nose; while the hoofs were like polished red pebbles, and even the shapely horns were tinged with that colour. Walking straight up to the old man, she began deliberately licking one of his ears with her big rough tongue, and in doing so knocked off his old rakish cap. Picking it up, he laughed like a child, and remarked, "She knows me, this one does – and she loikes me."

W. H. HUDSON

THERE was a great stir in the milk-house just after breakfast. The churn revolved as usual, but the butter would not come. Whenever this happened the dairy was paralysed. Squish, squash, echoed the milk in the great cylinder, but never arose the sound they waited for.

Dairyman Crick and his wife, the milkmaids Tess, Marian, Retty Priddle, Izz Huett, and the married ones from the cottages; also Mr Clare, Jonathan Kail, old Deborah, and the rest, stood gazing hopelessly at the churn; and the boy who kept the horse going outside put on moon-like eyes to show his sense of the situation. Even the melancholy horse himself seemed to look in at the window in inquiring despair at each walk round.

''Tis years since I went to Conjuror Trendle's son in Egdon – years!' said the dairyman bitterly. 'And he was nothing to what his father had been. I have said fifty times, if I have said once, that I don't believe in en. And I *don't* believe in en. But I shall have to go to 'n if he's alive. O yes, I shall have to go to 'n, if this sort of thing continnys!'

Even Mr Clare began to feel tragical at the dairyman's desperation.

'Conjuror Fall, t'other side of Casterbridge, that they used to call "Wide-O", was a very good man when I was a boy,' said Jonathan Kail. 'But he's rotten as touchwood by now.'

'My grandfather used to go to Conjuror Mynterne, out at Owlscombe, and a clever man a' were, so I've heard grandf'er say,' continued Mr Crick. 'But there's no such genuine folk about nowadays!'

Mrs Crick's mind kept nearer to the matter in hand.

'Perhaps somebody in the house is in love,' she said tentatively. 'I've heard tell in my younger days that that will cause it. Why, Crick – that maid we had years ago, do ye mind, and how the butter didn't come then –'

'Ah yes, yes! – but that isn't the rights o't. It had nothing to do with the love-making. I can mind all about it – 'twas the damage to the churn.'

He turned to Clare.

'Jack Dollop, a 'hore's-bird of a fellow we had here as milker at one time, sir, courted a young woman over at Mellstock, and deceived her as he had deceived many afore. But he had another sort o' woman to reckon wi' this time, and it was not the girl herself. One Holy Thursday, of all days in the almanack, we was here as we mid be now, only there was no churning in hand, when we zid the girl's mother coming up to the door, wi' a great brass-mounted umbrella in her hand that would ha' felled an ox, and saying, "Do Jack Dollop work here? – because I want him! I have a big bone to pick with he, I can assure 'n!" And some way behind her mother walked Jack's young woman, crying bitterly into her handkercher. "O Lard, here's a time!" said Jack, looking out o' winder at 'em. "She'll murder me! Where shall I get – where shall I –? Don't tell her where I be!" And with that he scrambled into the churn through the trap-door, and shut himself inside, just as the young woman's mother busted into the milk-house. "The villain – where is he?" says she, "I'll claw his face for'n, let me only catch him!" Well, she hunted about everywhere, ballyragging Jack by side and by seam, Jack lying a'most stifled inside the churn, and the poor maid – or young woman rather – standing at the door crying her eyes out. I shall never forget it, never! 'Twould have melted a marble stone! But she couldn't find him nowhere at all.'

The dairyman paused, and one or two words of comment came from the listeners.

Dairyman Crick's stories often seemed to be ended when they were not really so, and strangers were betrayed into premature interjections of finality; though old friends knew better. The narrator went on –

'Well, how the old woman should have had the wit to guess it

I could never tell, but she found out that he was inside that there churn. Without saying a word she took hold of the winch (it was turned by handpower then), and round she swung him, and Jack began to flop about inside. "O Lard! stop the churn! let me out!" says he, popping out his head, "I shall be churned into a pummy!" (he was a cowardly chap in his heart, as such men mostly be). "Not till ye make amends for ravaging her virgin innocence!" says the old woman. "Stop the churn, you old witch!" screams he. "You call me old witch, do ye, you deceiver!" says she, "when ye ought to ha' been calling me mother-law these last five months!" And on went the churn, and Jack's bones rattled round again. Well, none of us ventured to interfere; and at last 'a promised to make it right wi' her. "Yes – I'll be as good as my word!" he said. And so it ended that day.'

THOMAS HARDY

120

BECKY was a good hand at butter-making. She turned the handle of the churn, and coaxed the fine yellow grains together to make the solid lump, with a murmur of magic words. Susan hovered near, but she was not allowed to touch, for sometimes an elfish spirit gets in the churn and only those with the charm can get the butter to come. So she muttered and mumbled alone, and sure enough the sound of the swish, swish, altered, little animal thuds were heard, and the miracle happened.

ALISON UTTLEY

CHURN, butter, dash,
Cow's gone to th' marsh;
Peter stands at th' toll gate
Beggin' butter for his cake;
Come, butter, come!

TRADITIONAL

THE even ash-leaf in my left hand,
The first man I meet shall be my husband.
The even ash-leaf in my glove,
The first I meet shall be my love.
The even ash-leaf in my breast,
The first man I meet's whom I love best.
The even ash-leaf in my hand,
The first I meet shall be my man.
Even ash, even ash, I pluck thee,
This night my true love for to see;
Neither in his rick nor in his rear,
But in the clothes he does every day wear.
Find even ash or four-leaved clover,
An' you'll see your true love before the day's over.

TRADITIONAL

A Church Romance

(Mellstock: circa 1835)

SHE turned in the high pew, until her sight
Swept the west gallery, and caught its row
Of music-men with viol, book, and bow
Against the sinking sad tower-window light.

She turned again; and in her pride's despite
One strenuous viol's inspirer seemed to throw
A message from his string to her below,
Which said: 'I claim thee as my own forthright!'

Thus their hearts' bond began, in due time signed.
And long years thence, when Age had scared Romance,
At some old attitude of his or glance
That gallery-scene would break upon her mind,
With him as minstrel, ardent, young, and trim,
Bowing 'New Sabbath' or 'Mount Ephraim'.

THOMAS HARDY

The Crow sat on the willow

THE Crow sat on the willow tree
  A lifting up his wings
And glossy was his coat to see
And loud the ploughman sings
I love my love because I know
The milkmaid she loves me
And hoarsely croaked the glossy crow
Upon the willow tree
I love my love the ploughman sung
And all the field wi' music rung

I love my love a bonny lass
She keeps her pails so bright
And blythe she t[r]ips the dewy grass
At morning and at night
A cotton drab her morning gown
Her face was rosey health
She traced the pastures up and down
And nature was her wealth
He sung and turned each furrow down
His sweethearts love in cotton gown

My love is young and handsome
As any in the Town
She's worth a Ploughman's ransom
In the drab cotton gown
He sung and turned his furrows o'er
And urged his Team along
While on the willow as before
The old crow croaked his song

The ploughman sung his rustic Lay
And sung of Phebe all the day

The crow was in love no doubt
And wi a many things
The ploughman finished many a bout
And lustily he sings
My love she is a milking maid
Wi red and rosey cheek
O' cotton drab her gown was made
I loved her many a week
His milking maid the ploughman sung
Till all the fields around him rung

JOHN CLARE

125

I F a girl walk backwards to a pear tree on Christmas Eve, and
walk round it three times, she will see the spirit or image of
the man who is to be her husband.

On Halloween people go out in the dark and pluck cabbage-
stalks. If on this eve you scatter seeds or ashes down a lane, and
a girl follows you in the direction in which you have gone, she
will be your wife.

If you eat an apple at midnight upon All Halloween, and,
without looking behind you, gaze into a mirror, you will see the
face of your future husband or wife.

On New Year's Eve three unmarried girls may adopt the
following plan in order to see the spirits of their future husbands.
Let them go into a room which has two doors, and set the table
with knives, forks, and plates for three guests, and let them wait

in the room till twelve o'clock at midnight, at which hour exactly
the spirits of their future husbands will come in at one door and
go out at the other.

Let a girl take the stone out of a plum, throw the stone in the
fire, and say these lines:

> If he loves me crack and fly,
> If he hates me burn and die.

Then let her mention the name of her sweetheart. If he loves her
the stone will crack and fly out of the fire. If he does not love her
it will quietly burn to ashes.

Upon St Mark's Eve, or upon Hallows Eve, at midnight let a
girl go to a 'four-lane-ends' or cross-way, taking some barley
with her, then let her sprinkle the barley and say:

> Barley I sow, barley I trow,
> Let him who will my husband be
> Come after me and mow.

Then the future husband will come after her with a scythe and
mow. Or the girl may sow hemp-seed in the garden and say:

> Hempseed I sow,
> Hempseed pray grow.

. . . On Midsummer Eve let a girl take a sprig of myrtle and lay it
in her Prayer Book upon the words of the marriage service, 'Wilt
thou have this man to be thy wedded husband?' Then let her
close the book, put it under her pillow, and sleep upon it. If her
lover will marry her the myrtle will be gone in the morning, but
if it remains in the book he will not marry her.

On Hallows Eve let a girl cross her shoes upon her bedroom
floor in the shape of a T and say these lines:

> I cross my shoes in the shape of a T,
> Hoping this night my true love to see,
> Not in his best or worst array,
> But in the clothes of every day.

Then let her get into bed backwards without speaking any more that night, when she will see her future husband in her dreams.

At a wedding let the bride pass small pieces of bride-cake through her wedding-ring, and give them to unmarried men and girls. If they put the pieces under their pillows for three nights, on the third night they will dream of their true lovers.

S. O. ADDY

My husband used to tell a tale about some simple servant girl what were a-setting on the side o' the road on her half day off, because she ha'n't nothing else to do, when a strange man come down the road leading a stallion. When he got up to her, he passed the time o' day with her, as country folk usually do, and were prepared to pass on. But she had other ideas, an' pretended to be frightened.

'Oh!' she said 'You're a strange man, you are. Oh! Oh! Oh! what shall I do?'

The man were took back, and the horse started rearing an' curvetting about an' he had a job to hold it. 'What d'yer mean?' he said.

'Oh, you ain't gooin' to interfere wi' me, a' yer, man?' she said, pretending to cry.

'Don't be so soft, wench,' he said, very nearly being swung off his feet with the horse's capers, 'Can't yer see as I'm got this 'ere 'oss to see arter?'

'Well,' said the girl tearfully 'you could tie it to a gate.'

KATE MARY EDWARDS

S HE was a hardy, weather-beaten, good-tempered girl, with cheeks as firm and red as apples, and eyes brown as ripe hazel nuts. She was as strong as a man, and could carry a young calf in her arms, or two brimming cans of milk with anybody. She could wash, bake, brew herb beer, harness the horses, milk the cows, and take a turn in the fields.

Dan was for ever teasing her, but she bore it all with cheerful grins. He told her that the farm lads were in love with her, that the barber had asked for a lock of her hair, and that the road-mender was waiting down on the road, sitting on a heap of stones for a glimpse of her.

She shook her head and repeated:

'Nobody doesna want me, I reckon, but Mr Right will come some day,' and she washed up the milk-cans and scalded the churns, and polished the little brass labels, planning in the meantime a new ribbon for her neck to wear the next time she went out.

*

. . . The smell of baking came in waves from the oven where Becky crouched, with her oven cloth, putting in a fresh batch. She took out the brown loaves and turned them upside down out of their tins. She tapped on the bottoms listening with her head on one side, as if she expected a little bread man to open the door of the loaf and walk out to her.

'I wish Mr Right would come along quick,' she thought as she placed the loaves in a row, and cut fresh lumps from the remaining dough to 'prove' on the rack over the oven.

A knife fell on the floor, and she picked it up. That was a sign a man was coming. If it had been a fork, a woman would be expected. A black soot had waved on the bar all the afternoon, a stranger was on the way. She took off her floury apron and put on a clean one. She straightened up the kitchen and tidied her hair. Then she went to the little looking-glass which hung on the wall, and gazed intently at herself. Rosy cheeks, brown eyes, thick brown hair, a large mouth. She sighed, 'I wish I wasn't so red, red hands and cheeks. Vinegar makes a body pale, but I can't abide the stuff.' She sighed and absent-mindedly broke off a piece of kissing crust which she laid aside for Susan, when she returned from school.

Roger barked and tugged at his chain, and she heard steps coming to the side door. It was the oatcake man; she was glad she had heeded the signs and redded up.

'Come in, Mister,' she cried when she saw him, and he entered the low door and took off his cap. He put his large basket, with its neat piles of brown oatcakes and cream honey-combed pikelets all covered with a white cloth, on the dresser end, and stood shyly by the door.

ALISON UTTLEY

The Bonny Labouring Boy

As I walked out one morning being in the blooming Spring,
I heard a lovely maid complain – so grievously she sing,
Saying – Cruel was my parents they did me so annoy,
And will not let me marry with my bonny labouring boy.

Young Johnny was my true love's name as you may plainly
    see,
My parents did employ him their labouring boy to be,
To harrow – reap – to sow the seed – to plough my father's
    land,
And soon I fell in love with him as you may understand.

My father stepped up one morning and he seized me by the
    hand,
He swore he'd send young Johnny unto some foreign land,
He locked me in my bedroom my comfort to annoy,
And to keep me there to weep and mourn for my bonny
    labouring boy.

My mother stepped up next morning these words to me did
    say,
Your father has intended to appoint your wedding day,
But I did not make no answer – nor I dared not complain,
But until I wed my labouring boy then single I'll remain.

Oh his cheeks are like the roses – his eyes as black as sloes,
He smiles in his behaviour wherever my love goes.
He's manly – neat and handsome – his skin as white as snow,
In spite of my parents with my labouring boy I'll go.

So fill this glass up to the brim – let the toast come early round,
Here's a health to the labouring boy that ploughs and sows the
   ground,
And when his work is over his home he will enjoy,
Oh how happy is the girl that weds with a bonny labouring
   boy.

TRADITIONAL

129
The Orphaned Old Maid

I wanted to marry, but father said, 'No –
   'Tis weakness in women to give themselves so;
If you care for your freedom you'll listen to me,
Make a spouse in your pocket, and let the men be.'

I spake on't again and again: father cried,
'Why – if you go husbanding, where shall I bide?
For never a home's for me elsewhere than here!'
And I yielded; for father had ever been dear.

But now father's gone, and I feel growing old,
And I'm lonely and poor in this house on the wold,
And my sweetheart that was found a partner elsewhere,
And nobody flings me a thought or a care.

THOMAS HARDY

I N his relations with the other men he was always kindly and jovial. He was a bachelor, a fact which the other farm hands were not slow to comment on. 'W'en be ye goin' to get married, Bill? You'd better 'urry up before it's too late,' or, 'Ol' Bill, 'e's afraid o' the women 'e is! 'E knows too much about 'em!' Walker only chuckled and said he had enough to do to look after himself. He did not add that he had an aged mother and sister to support.

CHRISTOPHER HOLDENBY

131

I N my descent I came upon an old man carrying home a bundle of wood. He appeared surprised when I told him that I understood labourers were better off in Northumberland than elsewhere. He said that they reckoned, when they had taken everything into consideration, that they did not get more than 12s. a week. He had never been married, but had lived in his old and miserable cot for twenty years. 'Why had he never cared to marry?'

'Because,' he replied, 'a woman in Northumberland's not worth house room. Why, you see, sir, she's out in the field all day, and knows nothing about housework. A man can do varra superior to the vast of them.'

RICHARD HEATH

'WHY, he never got married not afore he was – what now? – fifty, I reckon. An' then he married two sisters.'

Before I could vent my astonishment at this, Bettesworth explained, 'One of 'em first; an' when she died then he took t'other. The vicar, he was down on 'n for that; but Edmund says, "Well, if I didn't marry her, somebody else would."'

'You see,' I began, 'it's –'

'Illegal, en't it, sir? . . . Well, Edmund didn't care.'

'Well, but the vicar didn't marry 'em?'

'No, *he* wouldn't have no hand in 't. But Edmund never cared. He wanted her, an' he had her. I dunno 'ow they *did* git married though . . .

'He was always a quiet livin' man. He lived 'long o' he's sister an' brother. They growed up together, and he never parted from 'em; but they all lived together. Then when they died off he took a wife. Well, of course, he wanted some one to keep things together for 'n, 'r else I don't suppose he'd ever ha' got married. On'y when they died off, he hadn't got nobody to *do* for 'n like.'

GEORGE BOURNE

133

Dame Durden

DAME DURDEN kept five servant-maids
　　To carry the milking-pail,
She also kept five labouring men
　　To use the spade and flail:

'Twas Moll and Bet, Doll and Kit,
　　And Dorothy Draggletail,
John and Dick, Joe and Jack,
　　And Humphrey with his flail.
John kissed Molly,
　　Dick kissed Betty,
Joe kissed Dolly,
　　Jack kissed Kitty,
And Humphrey with his flail
　　Kissed Dorothy Draggletail,
And Kitty she was a charming maid to carry the milking-pail.

Dame Durden in the morn so soon
　　She did begin to call;
To rouse her servant-maids and men
　　She then began to bawl:
'Twas Moll and Bet, Doll and Kit,
　　And Dorothy Draggletail,
John and Dick, Joe and Jack,
　　And Humphrey with his flail.
John kissed Molly, etc.

'Twas on the morn of Valentine,
　　The birds began to prate,
Dame Durden's servant-maids and men
　　They all began to mate:
'Twas Moll and Bet, Doll and Kit,
　　And Dorothy Draggletail,
John and Dick, Joe and Jack,
　　And Humphrey with his flail.
John kissed Molly, etc.

TRADITIONAL

. . . and now as I had become a Man and what must I do now been about twenty four years of age, what did I do but followed the advice that is given to us in the Second Chapter of Genesis Verse twenty four Therefore shall a Man Leave his Father and Mother and Cleave unto His Wife and they shall be one flesh and now I Began to Make known Myself to this person and in Corse of time She became my Lawfull wife. It was the fourteenth day of January in the Year of our Lord one thousand eight Hundred and forty nine that we joined In holy Matrimony.

As Regards our Household stuf we had but very Little true I had a bed and I had a very good Family Bible and I had but very Little Money, Must I say Only three shillings not much to start in Life was it, Well now I will tell you how we trudged along we Lived with my father and Mother up to the following Mickalmas so we had a chance to gather a few sticks together and were very Comfortable with them. While we were Living with them Our Family Incresed and very fond of it we was for it was a Little Girl but my wife had a very hard time of it we had to Call the Docter in he said he would not give a farthing for her Life if it had Been an hour Later but by the Blessing of the Almighty she began to get Better and you may be sure that I was very pleased for I was as fond of my wife Has a Cat is of New Milk I felt as if I Dare not tell her how much I Loved her because I thought she Would be trespising on were I should be and that would be the Head of the house.

JAMES BOWD

THE main fact is that the two sexes, each engaged daily upon essential duties, stand on a surprising equality the one to the other. And where the men are so well aware of the women's experienced outlook, and the women so well aware of the men's, the affectation of ignorance might almost be construed as a form of immodesty, or at any rate as an imprudence. It would, indeed, be too absurd to pretend that these wives and mothers, who have to face every trial of life and death for themselves, do not know the things which obviously they cannot help knowing; too absurd to treat them as though they were all innocence, and timidity, and daintiness. No labouring man would esteem a woman for delicacy of that kind, and the women certainly would not like to be esteemed for it. Hence the sexes habitually meet on almost level terms. And the absence of convention extends to a neglect – nay, to a dislike – of ordinary graceful courtesies between them. So far as I have seen they observe no ceremonial. The men are considerate to spare women the more exhausting or arduous kinds of work; but they will let a woman open the door for herself, and will be careless when they are together who stands or who sits, or which of them walks on the inside of the path, or goes first into a gateway. And the women look for nothing different. They expect to be treated as equals. If a cottage woman found that a cottage man was raising his hat to her, she would be aflame with indignation, and would let him know very plainly indeed that she was not that sort of fine lady.

GEORGE BOURNE

'**D**'YOU know, sir, as they always used to say in the village
as how I was the happiest girl about, afore I got married.
I knows I used to be in the fields all day a-picking flowers and
a-listening to the birds singing and watching the lambs jump-
ing. They all used to call me "Merry Kate". But Bill – well, 'e's
my 'usband and the bes' man as I knows – but 'e jus' didn't
understand, and so 'e laughed me out on it all. An' then came
the time as 'e got into trouble and thought as I didn't know. Of
course I knowed, which only made it worse, for w'en 'e came
back that there drunk with despair I 'ad to preten' to be angry,
and all the time I was sorry. Well, all the natural life was kind o'
gone out o' me, and if I hadn't had God and His pries' to talk to,
I think I'd 'a died.'

CHRISTOPHER HOLDENBY

137

A man's work is from sun to sun
But a woman's work is never done.

THAT's a rhyme I heard a-many a time when I was young,
and as far as the women in the fen, like my mother was
concerned, there's no doubt it were a true saying. If life were
hard for the men, it were harder still for the women. They often
worked side by side with their menfolk in the fields all day, then
went home and while their husbands fed the pig or fetched a
yoke o' water, they'd get the meal going. But most men could
rest a little while after tea, at least in winter, but the mother had

to set about preparing for the next day, getting the children washed and off to bed, and making and mending clothes and what bits o' furniture and linen they had in the house. Then they'd have to be up with the lark in the morning to sweep and clean the house afore it were time to go to work again. Of course, not all the women worked all the time, but most of 'em worked on the land in the busy times, and some of 'em boasted about being able to do as much as a man at some jobs. There were a lot of jobs a woman's quick neat fingers could do better than a man's, but I di'n't like to see a woman gault-digging, though I have seen 'em a good many times and a lot o' women 'set off' the turf for their husbands in the turf fen.

Then they would always either be carrying a child, or else had just had a new baby, and very often they would have two or three that couldn't walk. They boasted about the size o' their families, and would be ever so proud to say they'd got seven or eight sons and four or five daughters. Feeding a family like that on ten shillings a week, which was what the father 'ould bring home, were a job in itself.

KATE MARY EDWARDS

138

W HEN they reached home they handed the half-sovereign straight over to their wives, who gave them back a shilling for the next week's pocket-money. That was the custom of the countryside. The men worked for the money and the women had the spending of it. The men had the best of the bargain. They earned their half-sovereign by hard toil, it is true, but in the open air, at work they liked and took an interest in, and in congenial company. The women, kept close at home, with cooking, cleaning, washing, and mending to do, plus their constant pregnancies and a tribe of children to look after, had also the worry of ways and means on an insufficient income.

Many husbands boasted that they never asked their wives what they did with the money. As long as there was food enough, clothes to cover everybody, and a roof over their heads, they were satisfied, they said, and they seemed to make a virtue of this and think what generous, trusting, fine-hearted fellows they were. If a wife got in debt or complained, she was told: 'You must larn to cut your coat accordin' to your cloth, my gal.' The coats not only needed expert cutting, but should have been made of elastic.

FLORA THOMPSON

139

'I recollect the women, they were always busy: they were never idle. There was always work to do: they would make string rugs, and the children they would get the hessian, or a new sugar-bag, cut strips, pull the string out and make a string-mat. Then there was the cloth mats, cut-up clothes what was discarded. They were washed, cut up into shreds; and then to make them look neat and smart they would buy a soldier's red coat. From that soldier's coat a heart was made in the centre of the rug, and at the far corners there was the diamonds. But the best ones of the lot were the wool-made rugs. They used to make the wool rugs because there was a lot of wool used at that time. You had long stockings and the children had little socks; and when they got worn at the foot they would re-foot these stockings. What wool was to spare went into making these wool-rugs. And when there was a cold winter, many a time that wool-rug was kept and put on the bed. But we didn't have hot-water bottles because there was so many in the bed. We kept each other warm. We lay pretty close together in the bed: there was several in one bed; because, you see, the people in the country, most people, had large families then.'

ARTHUR WELTON

140

GRANNY BOWLES lived next the old man, and used frequently to look in upon him and minister to his needs; and when he died she performed the duties usual in such cases. She had been midwife and nurse for many years. She performed the office of Lucina and Proserpine as well: she presided over births and deaths, too. She both helped a man into the world and helped him out of it; swaddled him in the beginning and shrouded him in the end; laughed at his birth and wept over his funeral; made him comfortable in each case, or tried hard to; at any time and all times, day or night, Sunday or weekday, she was at everyone's beck and call. She left her own household to attend to the needs of others; did many and various acts of kindness and real self-sacrifice without ever knowing it or caring about it, for she was not covetous of people's favour; whether you praised her or blamed her it made little difference; she was firm and unmoved through all, short and curt, strong-willed, and very individual.

She was very tall – six feet, or thereabout – lank and lean, stooping a little toward the last, of robust appearance. Her forehead was deeply grooved, her cheeks wrinkled, but fresh-looking; nose long, slightly Roman; high arched brows, grey eyes, lips thin, strained together; pointed chin, silver-grey hair carefully combed. She wore a woollen crossover, blue print apron, old-fashioned sun-bonnet, with a heavy pair of boots. She had lived a hard life, and brought up a large family. When she was young she worked on the farm in the fields, with a whole troop of girls beside. She was delighted to tell you all about the early days spent with the old companions – hard times they may have been, but pleasant they certainly were; it always is a joy to look back on past labours. It is work and hardship that brings out all that is finest in us, male or female. Those who do nothing have precious little retrospect; there is nothing to remember. It was of such as these Sallust was thinking in the 'Catiline' when he said, 'Their life and death are alike, for they are silent in each.'

After she married Bowles – she always spoke of, and addressed her husband as, Bowles – she still went out to work, and while she had infant children, too. As soon as these were big enough she took them out in the fields with her, wrapped them in a shawl, and set them down under the hedge while she worked away, as they did in olden times, which we learn from the description in 'Piers Plowman'. Her husband worked on the farm. He was cowman and general hand, and an excellent hedge-cutter. His complexion was almost blue with exposure; he was a hard worker, of strong principle, a dutiful husband and a stern parent. When the boys had been guilty of any offence, off came the belt, and they had it, buckle-end if the affair was serious. But the husband and father ranked second in the house; 'Nance' was the predominant figure there. It was not till middle age that she adopted the profession of midwife. Jacky Bridge's mother fulfilled the office before her. They had no certificates in those days, nor were doctors often called in to attend at births in country places, and accidents were rare. I have heard Granny Bowles declare she never had a bad case in her life.

ALFRED WILLIAMS

SNEEZE on Monday, sneeze for danger,
Sneeze on Tuesday, kiss a stranger,
Sneeze on Wednesday, get a letter,
Sneeze on Thursday, something better,
Sneeze on Friday, sneeze for sorrow,
Saturday, see your true-love to-morrow.

TRADITIONAL

142

All of a Row

THE corn is all ripe and the reapings begin,
The fruits of the earth, O we gather them in;
At morning so early the reaphooks we grind,
And away to the fields for to reap and to bind.
The foreman goes first in the hot summer glow,
And sings with a laugh, my lads, of a row.
Then all of a row!
Then all of a row!
And tonight we will sing,
Boys, all of a row.

'We're in', says the Catchpole, behind and before,
'We'll have a fresh edge and a sheaf or two more';
The master stands back for to see us behind;
'Well done, honest fellows, bring the sheaves to the bind.
Well done, honest fellows, pare up your first brink
You shall have a fresh edge and a half pint to drink.'
Then all of a row! etc.

And so we go on through the heat of the day,
Some reaping, some binding, all merry and gay,
We'll reap and we'll bind, we will whistle and sing,
Unflagging until the last sheaf we bring in;
It's all our enjoyment wherever we go,
To work and to sing, brothers, all of a row.
Then all of a row! etc.

Our day's work is done, to the farmhouse we steer,
To eat a good supper and drink humming beer;
We wish the good farmer all the blessings in life,
And drink to his health, and as well to his wife.
God prosper the grain for next harvest we sow,
And again in the arrish we'll sing, boys, hallo.
Then all of a row! etc.

TRADITIONAL

143
'Taking the Harvest'

HERE is an actual contract for 'taking the harvest': it was drawn up at Grove Farm by old George Rope some time during the last quarter of the nineteenth century. The confusion of person in the first sentence is understandable as the contract was written out in Old George's hand; and as the sole contracting party on one side it was easier for him to write *my* than the more impersonal, if more accurate, *the master's* or some other third person equivalent.

We the undermentioned agree to cut and secure all the corn grown on the farm in a workmanlike manner to my satisfaction; make bottoms of stacks; cover up when required; hoe the turnips twice and turn or lift the barley once; turn the pease once – each man to find a gaveller. Should any man lose any time through sickness he is to throw back 2s. per day to the Company and receive account at harvest. Should any man lose any time through drunkenness he is to forfeit 5s. to the Company.

Joe Levett
Jas. Hammond
R. French
Jn Keable
Joe Row
Samuel Ling

Allowances to each man:
    1 Coomb of Wheat at 20s.
    3 Bushels of Malt – gift
    1 lb of Mutton to each man instead of dinner
    2½ lbs of Mutton at 4d. a lb every Friday

David Ling, lad:	To receive half as much as the other men make in their harvest and half their allowances
Boy Woodbridge:	½ Bushel of Malt: 2/6 a week during harvest
Boy Leggett:	3s. a week during harvest. 1 Bushel of Malt

        92 acres at 6s. 6d.   £29. 18 0
                                          2 0
                                  ‾‾‾‾‾‾‾‾‾‾‾‾
                                  £30 0. 0

GEORGE EWART EVANS

I N the fields where the harvest had begun all was bustle and activity. At that time the mechanical reaper with long, red revolving arms like windmill sails had already appeared in the locality; but it was looked upon by the men as an auxiliary, a farmer's toy; the scythe still did most of the work and they did not dream it would ever be superseded. So while the red sails revolved in one field and the youth on the driver's seat of the machine called cheerily to his horses and women followed behind to bind the corn into sheaves, in the next field a band of men would be whetting their scythes and mowing by hand as their fathers had done before them.

With no idea that they were at the end of a long tradition, they still kept up the old country custom of choosing as their leader the tallest and most highly skilled man amongst them, who was then called 'King of the Mowers'. For several harvests in the 'eighties they were led by the man known as Boamer. He had served in the Army and was still a fine, well-set-up young fellow with flashing white teeth and a skin darkened by fiercer than English suns.

With a wreath of poppies and green bindweed trails around his wide, rush-plaited hat, he led the band down the swathes as they mowed and decreed when and for how long they should halt for 'a breather' and what drinks should be had from the yellow stone jar they kept under the hedge in a shady corner of the field. They did not rest often or long; for every morning they set themselves to accomplish an amount of work in the day that they knew would tax all their powers till long after sunset. 'Set yourself more than you can do and you'll do it' was one of their maxims, and some of their feats in the harvest field astonished themselves as well as the onlooker.

FLORA THOMPSON

THE oats have been trampled by rain, and two men are reaping it by hand. They are not men of the farm, but rovers who take their chance and have done other things than reaping in their time. One is a Hampshire man, but fought with the Wiltshires against 'Johnny Boer' – he liked the Boers . . . 'they were very much like a lot of working men . . . We never beat 'em . . . No, we never beat 'em.' He is a man of heroic build; tall, lean, rather deep-chested than broad-shouldered, narrow in the loins, with goodly calves which his old riding breeches perfectly display; his head is small, his hair short and crisp and fair, his cheeks and neck darkly tanned, his eye bright blue and quick-moving, his features strong and good, except his mouth, which is over large and loose; very ready to talk, which he does continually in a great proud male voice, however hard he is working. A man as lean and hard and bright as his reaping hook. First he snicks off a dozen straws and lays them on the ground for a bond, then he slashes fast along the edge of the corn for two or three yards, gathers up what is cut into his hook and lays it across the straws: when a dozen sheaves are prepared in the same way he binds them with bonds and builds them into a stook of two rows leaning together. It is impossible to work faster and harder than he does in cutting and binding; only at the end of each dozen sheaves does he stand at his full height, straight as an ash, and laugh, and round off what he has been saying even more vigorously than he began it. Then crouching again he slays twelve other sheaves. Then he goes over to the four-and-a-half-gallon cask in the hedge: it is 'fuel' that he likes, and he pays for it himself.

EDWARD THOMAS

'THE hell of the life was the harvest. You'd see some lovely paintings of men at harvest. Well! I was sixteen when I was told I had got to do me harvest, with the other men. Well! that meant an outlay. I had to buy a scythe. Then I had to buy a "tommy-hawk" – to rake the corn in. On top of that, I had to buy a beer bottle. No man could harvest unless he had a gallon of beer a day. The brewers used to come round at a cheap rate: nine gallons for four-and-six, paid for after harvest. That was a special harvest brew, and I don't mind telling you if that brew was brewed today and they gave a man a breathing test, that 'ud bust the ruddy bag.

'You'd start mowing at half-past six in the morning. You'd wipe the last lot of sweat off about half-past eight at night. And how much do you think you would earn? Five shillings. That was ten shillings an acre. Well! after you'd mown, you'd got to tie it up in sheaves; then set it up in shocks. In those days every man wore two pairs of trousers; one back to the front, because they'd wear out the knees in a couple of days. It were the first three days which were hell. After that your muscles got used to it. I seen a strong man stand up and howl like a child, especially if there were a lot of green stuff in the corn that made it harder. See? Clean corn was all right, because your scythe would go through it, but if there was a lot of bindweed or scratch weed, that was like pulling a truck off a railway line. Once your muscles got used to it, it was nothing. What would a man say today if he was at work in the harvest field and his wife came along with a big bottle of white oils – horse oils; a shilling a pint from the chemist's. She'd come along and rub his loins, because he was in such agony.'

W. H. BARRETT

REAPING. Rye. The tall rye, thin straw, dry hiss of the wind over, thin air and grain partly exposed. Reaper holds back the rye with left hand and strikes near the ground. Large shocks and the ears curve drooping slightly, not upright like wheat. More of a grassy look.

RICHARD JEFFERIES

148

THE reapers leave their beds before the sun
     And gleaners follow when home toils are done
To pick the littered ear the reaper leaves
And glean in open fields among the sheaves
The ruddy child nursed in the lap of care
In toils rude ways to do its little share
Beside its mother poddles oer the land
Sun burnt and stooping with a weary hand
Picking its tiney glean of corn or wheat
While crackling stubbles wound its legs and feet

JOHN CLARE

AFTER the harvest had been carried from the fields, the women and children swarmed over the stubble picking up the ears of wheat the horse-rake had missed. Gleaning, or 'leazing', as it was called locally.

Up and down and over and over the stubble they hurried, backs bent, eyes on the ground, one hand outstretched to pick up the ears, the other resting on the small of the back with the 'handful'. When this had been completed, it was bound round with a wisp of straw and erected with others in a double rank, like the harvesters erected their sheaves in shocks, beside the leazer's water-can and dinner-basket. It was hard work, from as soon as possible after daybreak until nightfall, with only two short breaks for refreshment; but the single ears mounted, and a woman with four or five strong, well-disciplined children would carry a good load home on the head every night. And they enjoyed doing it, for it was pleasant in the fields under the pale blue August sky, with the clover springing green in the stubble and the hedges bright with hips and haws and feathery with traveller's joy. When the rest-hour came, the children would wander off down the hedgerows gathering crab-apples or sloes, or searching for mushrooms, while the mothers reclined and suckled their babes and drank their cold tea and gossiped or dozed until it was time to be at it again.

FLORA THOMPSON

Gleaning

ALONG the baulk the grasses drenched in dews
Soak through the morning gleaners' clumsy shoes,
And cloying cobwebs trammel their brown cheeks
While from the shouldering sun the dewfog reeks.
Now soon begun, on ground where yesterday
The rakers' warning-sheaf forbade their way,
Hard clacking dames in great white hoods make haste
To cram their lapbags with the barley waste,
Scrambling as if a thousand were but one,
Careless of stabbing thistles. Now the sun
Gulps up the dew and dries the stubs, and scores
Of tiny people trundle out of doors
Among the stiff stalks, where the scratched hands ply –
Red ants and blackamoors and such as fly;
Tunbellied, too, with legs a finger long,
The spider harvestman; the churlish strong
Black scorpion, prickled earwig, and that mite
Who shuts up like a leaden shot in fright
And lies for dead. And still before the rout
The young rats and the fieldmice whisk about
And from the trod whisp out the leveret darts,
Bawled at by boys that pass with blundering carts
Top-heavy to the red-tiled barns. – And still
The children feed their corn-sacks with good will,
And farmwives ever faster stoop and flounce.
The hawk drops down a plummet's speed to pounce
The nibbling mouse or resting lark away.
The lost mole tries to pierce the mattocked clay
In agony and terror of the sun.

The dinner hour and its grudged leisure won,
All sit below the pollards on the dykes,
Rasped with the twinge of creeping barley spikes.
Sweet beyond telling now the small beer goes
From the hooped hardwood bottles, the wasp knows,
And even hornets whizz from the eaten ash;
Then crusts are dropt and switches snatched to slash,
While safe in shadow of the apron thrown
Aside the bush which years before was grown
To snap the poacher's nets, the baby sleeps.

Now toil returns, in red-hot fluttering light,
And far afield the weary rabble creeps,
Oft happening blind wheat, black among the white,
That smutches where it touches quick as soot; –
Oft gaping where the landrail seems afoot,
Who with such magic throws his baffling speech
Far off he sounds when scarce beyond arm's reach.
The dogs are left to mind the morning's gain,
But squinting knaves can slouch to steal the grain.
Close to the farm the fields are gleaned agen,
Where the boy droves the turkey and white hen
To pick the shelled sweet corn, their hue and cry
Answers the gleaners' gabble; and sows trudge by
With little pigs to play and rootle there,
And all the fields are full of din and blare.

So steals the time past, so they glean and gloat;
The hobby-horse whirs round, the moth's dust coat
Blends with the stubble, scarlet soldiers fly
In airy pleasure; but the gleaners' eye
Sees little but their spoils, or robin-flower
Ever on tenterhooks to shun the shower, –
Their weather-prophet never known astray;

When he folds up, then towards the hedge glean they.
But now the dragon of the skies droops, pales,
And wandering in the wet grey western vales
Stumbles, and passes, and the gleaning's done.
The farmer with fat hares slung on his gun
Gives folks goodnight, as down the ruts they pull
The creaking two-wheeled handcarts bursting full,
And whimpering children cease their teazing squawls
While left alone the supping partridge calls –
Till all at home is stacked from mischief's way,
To thrash and dress the first wild windy day;
And each good wife crowns weariness with pride,
With such small winnings more than satisfied.

EDMUND BLUNDEN

151

*M*RS SMART, wife of — Smart, Calne, Wiltshire, stone-mason, examined. I went out leasing (gleaning) this autumn for three weeks, and was very lucky: I got, six bushels of corn. I got up at two o'clock in the morning, and got home at seven at night. My other girls, aged 10, 15, and 18, went with me. We leased in the neighbourhood, and sometimes as far as seven miles off.

I have had 13 children, and have brought seven up. I have been accustomed to work in the fields at hay-time and harvest. Sometimes I have had my mother, and sometimes my sister, to take care of the children, or I could not have gone out. I have gone to work at seven in the morning till six in the evening; in harvest sometimes much later, but it depends on circumstances. Women with a family cannot be ready so soon as the men, and must be home earlier, and therefore they don't work so many hours. In making hay I have been strained with the work: I have felt it sometimes for weeks; so bad sometimes I could not get out of my chair. In leasing, in bringing home the corn, I have hurt my head, and have been made deaf by it. Often, out of the hay-fields, myself and my children have come home with our things quite wet through: I have gone to bed for an hour for my things to get a little dry, but have had to put them on again when quite wet. My health is very good now.

I generally had 10d. a-day, sometimes as much as 1s. a-day. My husband earns 15s. a-week, but his employment is not regular. Our boys are brought up to their father's work.

We pay 7l. a-year rent for our cottage and large garden. There are three rooms in the cottage; two bed-rooms, in which we have three beds; and we find great difficulty in sleeping our family. When we wash our sheets, we must have them dry again by night. In the garden we raise plenty of potatoes. We have about a shilling's worth of meat a-week; a pig's milt sometimes; a pound or three-quarters of a pound of suet. Seven gallons of bread a-week; sometimes a little pudding on a Sunday. I can cook a little. I was, before I married, housemaid, and afterwards cook in a family.

152

IN 1856, I entered upon my first harvest. During the wheat-cutting I made bonds for the binders. There were no reaping machines in those days, the corn all having to be cut by the scythe. Women were engaged to tie up the corn, and the little boys made bonds with which to tie the corn. For this work I received 3d. per day, or at the rate of 1s. 6d. per week.

When the wheat was carted I led the horse and shouted to the loaders to hold tight when the horse moved. When this work was finished and there was nothing further for me to do, I went gleaning with my mother. In those days it was the custom for the poor to glean the wheatfields after they had been cleared. This was a help to the poor, for it often provided them with a little bread during the winter months, when they would not have had half enough to eat had it not been that they were allowed to glean. The men used to thresh the corn with a flail, dress it and clean it, and send it to the mill to be ground into meal. The rules for gleaning were very amusing. No one was allowed in the field while there was a sheaf of corn there, and at a given hour the farmer would open the gate and remove the sheaf, and shout 'All on.' If anyone went into the field before this was done the rest would 'shake' the corn she had gleaned.

This was a happy time for the women and children. At the conclusion of the harvest they would have what was called a gleaners' frolic.

GEORGE EDWARDS

153

THE reaping-machine left the fallen corn behind it in little heaps, each heap being of the quantity for a sheaf; and upon these the active binders in the rear laid their hands – mainly women, but some of them men in print shirts, and trousers supported round their waists by leather straps, rendering useless the two buttons behind, which twinkled and bristled with sunbeams at every movement of each wearer, as if they were a pair of eyes in the small of his back.

But those of the other sex were the most interesting of this company of binders, by reason of the charm which is acquired by woman when she becomes part and parcel of outdoor nature, and is not merely an object set down therein as at ordinary times. A field-man is a personality afield; a field-woman is a portion of the field; she has somehow lost her own margin, imbibed the essence of her surrounding, and assimilated herself with it.

The women – or rather girls, for they were mostly young – wore drawn cotton bonnets with great flapping curtains to keep off the sun, and gloves to prevent their hands being wounded by the stubble. There was one wearing a pale pink jacket, another in a cream-coloured tight-sleeved gown, another in a petticoat as red as the arms of the reaping-machine; and others, older, in the brown-rough 'wropper' or over-all – the old-established and most appropriate dress of the field-woman, which the young ones were abandoning. This morning the eye returns involuntarily to the girl in the pink cotton jacket, she being the most flexuous and finely-drawn figure of them all. But her bonnet is pulled so far over her brow that none of her face is disclosed while she binds, though her complexion may be guessed from a stray twine or two of dark brown hair which extends below the curtain of her bonnet. Perhaps one reason why she seduces casual attention is that she never courts it, though the other women often gaze around them.

Her binding proceeds with clock-like monotony. From the sheaf last finished she draws a handful of ears, patting their tips with her left palm to bring them even. Then stooping low she moves forward, gathering the corn with both hands against her knees, and pushing her left gloved hand under the bundle to meet the right on the other side, holding the corn in an embrace like that of a lover. She brings the ends of the bond together, and kneels on the sheaf while she ties it, beating back her skirts now and then when lifted by the breeze. A bit of her naked arm is visible between the buff leather of the gauntlet and the sleeve of her gown; and as the day wears on its feminine smoothness becomes scarified by the stubble, and bleeds.

THOMAS HARDY

ALSO, when harvest was come, she work'd in the field with
      her sickle;
   Wheat, and barley, and beans fell to the sweep of her blade:
She could keep up with the men at reaping, and binding, and
      stacking;
   She could keep up with the men; she could leave laggards
   behind.
All through the sultry days, in the silent ranks of the reapers,
   Dorothy wrought like a man, keeping her time with the best;
Earning her harvest wage – for her wages were doubled in
      harvest;
   Earning her bacon and bread under the hazels at noon.
Brown grew her handsome face, her bare arms brown as the
      chestnut;
   She too, a labourer still, wrought in the sweat of her brow;
But, with her hair tied up in a handkerchief under her bonnet,
   And with her lilac frock kilted up gaily behind,
She was a pleasure to see; and there was not a man of her
      fellows
   Would not have snatch'd, if he dared, Dorothy's
   hard-working hand.

                                        A. J. MUNBY

THE sight of the men, one following the other across the field
      in a jagged line as they cut down the ripe corn with wide
sweeps of the scythe, made a fine picture of effort strenuous and

combined. The place is pretty too, with the windmill in the background, and the heat-haze softened the scene, keeping it in tone and making it restful. One of the features of these mowings is the almost invariable presence of a man with a dog – someone in the village who is fond of a bit of sport. As the mowers approach the end of a stretch a bunny or two will bolt, and be swept up by the dog before it can win the shelter of the hedge.

RIDER HAGGARD

156

T EN men and a boy in the wheat each with a big stick, shouting like war, the reaping machine still in the corner. He goes, 'Let the little imp go.' Here's a chase in the stubble. Stick misses. One huge fellow catches his foot in a sheaf and goes head over heels. Rabbit doubles back to the wheat. One lying on sheaf, brown and brown-grey, red handkerchief by it, drops of red blood on the yellow straw.

RICHARD JEFFERIES

The Reaphook and Sickle

Come all you lads and lasses, together let us go
Into some pleasant cornfield our courage for to show,
With the reaphook and the sickle so well we clear the land,
The farmer says, 'Well done, my lads, here's liquor at your
command.'

By daylight in the morning when birds so sweetly sing –
They are such charming creatures they make the valley ring –
We will reap and scrape together till Phoebus do go down,
With the good old leathern bottle and beer that is so brown.

Then in comes lovely Nancy the corn all for to lay,
She is my charming creature, I must begin to pray;
See how she gathers it, binds it, she folds it in her arms,
Then gives it to some waggoner to fill a farmer's barns.

Now harvest's done and ended, the corn secure from harm,
All for to go to market, boys, we must thresh in the barn.
Here's a health to all you farmers, likewise to all you men,
I wish you health and happiness till harvest comes again.

TRADITIONAL

'Of all the jobs I ever did as a boy . . . that were the hardest – *and* the sweatiest. In them days we used to tread the corn down in the barns with hosses. The loads were brought in at the mainst'y doors and forked up into the bays till the wheat mounted nigh up to the rafters. And they used to make boys like me ride the hosses round an' round, treadin' down the corn. Hours at harvest-time 'ld be almost as long as the day itself; and there we'd be, from half-past five of a mornin' till half-past eight of a night – and sometimes later – tuggin' at the old mare's head to pull her out of the straw. Eightpence a day was what us boys got for the job: that's double pay, of course, bein' harvest. Well, you know for yourself what it's like walkin' about on top of a stack when they're a-buildin' it: you sink in to your knees and keep on liftin' your feet till it seems as if they're made of lead. So you can just imagine what it was like for 'osses – and some of the best an' biggest on the farm at that. They'd soon get to be all of a lather. But round an' round they had to goo, up to their bellies in the straw most of the time; and we had to keep on coaxin' 'em and tuggin' at 'em for all we was worth. If we so much as let 'em stop for a moment, it was 'Hi! what are you a-doin' up there?' I can tell you, I *cried* at that job.

'Sometimes the mare would be nigh standin' on her hind legs, staggerin' about, and me tryin' all the time to keep her on the move. You see, treading the corn like this didn't crush the kernels, but drove a lot of 'em out of the husks, and of course the threshers liked that. Fast as the men had pitched up one load, another 'ld draw into the barn; and presently the 'oss and me was right up there under the roof, in the dark, sneezin' and splutterin' fit to bust. Once the mare was up, there she'd have to stay till the job was done – 'cause though you could get her down, how was you to get her up again? Two or three days she'd be up there, an' more if bad weather held up the carting. Sometimes it 'ld get so dark – well, I *couldn't* see; but I had to keep on keepin' on, so long as they was a-bringin' in new loads and torsin' 'em up from the mainst'y. And when it was all done at last, the only way of getting the old mare down was to drag her by the halter, so's she slid on her hoofs and belly, clatterin' an' kickin' up no end of a shine. You can bet a hoss had to be purty tough to stand it. Why, 'twould be called cruelty to-day – 'twouldn't be allowed. But such things weren't thought nothin' of, them days.'

MARK THURSTON

159

I T is the custom in Nottinghamshire to make the last sheaf of the harvest big in order to ensure a good crop the next year. The youngest boys in the village ride home on the last load of wheat, the wagon being decorated with branches of trees. Apples and buckets of cold water are thrown over the boys as they ride home singing the following harvest song:

> Mr — is a good man,
> He lets us ride his harvest home,
> He gives us apples, he gives us ale,
> We wish his heart may never fail.
> *With a hip, hip, hurrah,*
> *A dry wagon, a dry wagon,*
> *A sup of cold water*
> *To keep it from swagging.*

God bless these horses that trail us home,
For they've had many a weary bone,
They've rent their clothes and torn their skin,
All for to get this harvest in.
With a hip, hip, hurrah, etc.

S. O. ADDY

160

The Ploughshare

THE sun has gone down and the sky it looks red
Down on my soft pillow where I lay my head,
When I open my eyes for to see the stars shine
Then the thoughts of my true love run into my mind.

The sap has gone down and the leaves they do fall,
To hedging and ditching our farmers they'll call.
We will trim up their hedges we will cut down their wood
And the farmers they'll all say our faggots run good.

Now hedging being over then sawing draws near
We will send for the sawyer the woods for to clear.
And after he has sawed them and tumbled them down
Then there he will flaw them all on the cold ground.

When sawing is over then seedtime comes round,
See our teams they are already preparing the ground,
Then the man with his seed-lip he'll scatter the corn
Then the harrows they will bury it to keep it from harm.

Now seedtime being over then haying draws near,
With our scythes, rakes, and pitch-forks those meadows to
    clear.
We will cut down their grass, boys, and carry it away,
We will first call it green grass and then call it hay.

When haying is over then harvest draws near
We will send to our Brewer to brew us strong beer,
And in brewing strong beer, boys, we will cut down their corn
And we'll take it to the barn, boys, to keep it from harm.

Now harvest being over bad weather comes on,
We will send for the thresher to thresh out our corn.
His hand-staff he'll handle, his swingel he'll swing,
Till the very next harvest we'll all meet again.

Now since we have brought this so cheerfully around
We will send for the jolly ploughman to plough up the ground.
See the boy with his whip and the man to his plough
Here's a health to the jolly ploughmen that plough up the
    ground.

Toast: Here's success to the bright ploughshare and may it
    never rust.

Company: May the ploughshare never rust.

TRADITIONAL

Most employers, when harvest was over, gave a supper for their workers; the man for whom my parents worked for over thirty years gave one jointly with two or three other farmers. A big brick and tiled barn was swept out, the cobwebs were brushed down from the rafters, rows of trestle tables were set up down the middle of the building and a platform was put up at one end. Plenty of beer was brought in and huge joints of roast beef and pork provided the main part of the supper which was served by the labourer's wives, a man at each table carving the joints.

When the meal was over 'our' farmer and the others who were giving the feast with him, each made a little speech thanking everyone for all the work that had been done and when each man had had his say there would be loud shouts of 'For he's a jolly good fellow, and so say all of us.' – though probably only the day before some of the workers had been calling him, under their breath, anything but a good fellow. Then some of the older harvestmen used to get up and make a speech, though what they said could hardly be called great oratory. One old man, I remember, could only just manage to stammer out:

'If yew young fellas was to dew a bit more like our good Ma-aster dew, there wouldn't be so many on yer dew as yew dew dew' before he sat down overcome by his great effort.

The speeches ended, Fiddler Brown and an accordion player named Loggins would then strike up a tune and everyone would march round the tables singing

Hayman, Strawman, Raggedy-Arse, Maliserman

and this would start the entertainment part of the evening. Plenty of comic songs were sung, plenty of beer was drunk and there was dancing, too, one man at least being sure to do a

Broomstick Dance by holding a besom in front of him and moving forwards, at each step putting first one leg and then the other over the broom. This needed some doing, especially if the dancer had a good lot of beer in him, if he was not to trip and fall flat on his face.

ARTHUR RANDELL

162

A Harvest Song

WHO knocks there?
    Poor Peg.
What's poor Peg want?
A shroud to wrap poor Tom in.
What's poor Tom dead?
Yes.
When did er die?
Yesterday in the morning gray
Parted poor Tom and I
I heard a bird singing in the wood
Poor Tom was like to die
Now what shall us do
For poor Tom's sake
For he was a right honest man
We'll take this cup and drink him up
And so shall everyone
Ring a right and do no wrong.
Poor Tom is dead and gone
Boom (*drink*) Boom (*drink*) Boom (*drink*)

TRADITIONAL

H ERE's a health to the world, as round as a wheel,
Death is a thing we all shall feel;
If life were a thing that money could buy
The rich would live and the poor would die.

TRADITIONAL

164

M Y fondness for study began to decline on mixing more
into company [with] young chaps of loose habits that
began by force & growing into a custom was continued by
choice till it became wild & irregular   Poetry was for a season
thrown by   these habits were gotten when the fields were enclosed mixing among a motley set of labourers that always
follow the news of such employments   I usd to work at setting
down fencing & planting quick-lines with partners whose whole
study was continual striving how to get beer & the bottle was the
general theme from week-end to week-end   such as had got
drunk the oftenest fancied themselves the best fellows & made a
boast of it as a fame but I was not such a drinker as to make a
boast of it   though I joined my sixpence towards the bottle as
often as the rest I often missed the tot that was handed round for
my constitution would not have borne it   Saturday nights usd to
be what they calld randy nights which was all meeting together
at the public-house to drink & sing & every new beginner had to
spend a larger portion than the rest which they calld 'colting' a
thing common in all sorts of labour

JOHN CLARE

The Topers Rant

COME come my old crones & gay fellows
 That loves to drink ale in a horn
We'll sing racey songs now we're mellow
Which topers sung ere we were born
For our bottle kind fate shall be thanked
& line but our pockets with brass
We'll sooner suck ale through a blanket
Then thimbles of wine from a glass

Away with your proud thimble glasses
Of wine foreign nations supply
We topers neer drink to the lasses
Over draughts scarce enough for a flye
Club us with the hedger & ditcher
Or beggar that makes his own horn
To join us oer bottle or pitcher
Foaming oer with the essence of corn

We care not with whom we get tipsey
Or where with brown stout we regale
We'll weather the storm with a gipsey
If he be a lover of ale
We'll weather the toughest storm weary
Although we get wet to the skin
If the outside our cottage looks dreary
We're warm & right happy within

We'll sit till the bushes are dropping
Like the spout of a watering pan
For till the drams drank theres no stopping
We'll keep up the ring to a man

We'll sit till dame nature is feeling
The breath of our stingo so warm
& bushes & trees begin reeling
In our eyes like to ships in a storm

We'll sit from three hours before seven
When larks wake the morning to dance
Till nights sutty brood of eleven
When witches ride over to france
We'll sit it in spite of the weather
Till we tumble our length on the plain
When the morning shall find us together
To play the game over again

                                        JOHN CLARE

166

Duʀɪɴɢ my inquiries in the West of England, I was frequently told by farmers and others that the agricultural
labourers were very dissipated in their habits. There is a kind of
mournful irony in talking of the 'dissipation' of a man on 9s. a
week. But I was assured, that to the extent permitted by their
wretched wages, the labourers were, in very many cases, drunk-
en and improvident in their habits. As to the general charge of
drunkenness, I am bound to say, that during the whole course of
my inquiries, both out of doors and in the cottages of the
labourers, I never met with an intoxicated farm labourer. I was
asked to believe that what caused the extreme destitution of the
labourers was not so much their wretched wages as habits of
intemperance and improvidence.

                                        F. G. HEATH

THERE was another old fellow who used to be employed about the village, road-mending with Jacky before mentioned. He was known as 'Baby, dear'. This was Johnny Garret, who lived in the little old thatched cottage that stood by the church, but which is demolished now. His chief vocations in life had been those of hedge-cutter, haymaker, and harvester – three of the very finest trades since the days of Adam. When these failed or were out of season, he 'snopped' stones by the roadside, pared the borders, cleaved trenches to carry off the water, and so on. He was small in stature, very thin, long nose, fierce ferret eyes, heavy brows, and thick grey hair. He brought four hammers to the stone-breaking – a sledge, a middle-sized one, and two smaller. After sledging the heap, or a part of it, he knelt on an old sack and 'snopped' away. We children helped, or hindered him, taking a hammer each, till one or the other received a clout, then the old man sent us all going. Johnny's failing was the ale; he must have a drop of the liquor, though he did not imbibe much – a pint would make the old fellow tipsy. After partaking of a drop he became very serious and talkative, addressing himself most pertinently, and answering the questions with great ceremony. The matter was usually cut short by the appearance of his wife Amy, who hauled him off roughly, and slammed up the cottage door with violence. Both lived to a ripe old age and received the parish pay – two shillings a week, and two half-gallon loaves of bread with it.

ALFRED WILLIAMS

Shortening Days at the Homestead

THE first fire since the summer is lit, and is smoking into
.   the room:
   The sun-rays thread it through, like woof-lines in a loom.
   Sparrows spurt from the hedge, whom misgivings appal
That winter did not leave last year for ever, after all.
   Like shock-headed urchins, spiny-haired,
   Stand pollard willows, their twigs just bared.

Who is this coming with pondering pace,
Black and ruddy, with white embossed,
His eyes being black, and ruddy his face,
And the marge of his hair like morning frost?
   It's the cider-maker,
   And appletree-shaker,
And behind him on wheels, in readiness,
His mill, and tubs, and vat, and press.

THOMAS HARDY

HERE's to the old apple tree,
   Bud and blow,
And bear apples enow,
Hats-full, caps-full, three bushel bags-full
And some for the boys to steal.

TRADITIONAL

Here's to the inside of a loaf and the outside of a gaol,
A good beefsteak and a quart of good ale.

TRADITIONAL

171

JAMES PARSONS, a very infirm man, over seventy, asthmatic and failing, has been a labourer all his life, and for the greater part of it on one farm. His father was famed through the whole country side as 'The Singing Machine', he was considered to be inexhaustible. Alas! he is no more, and his old son shakes his head and professes to have but half the ability, memory, and musical faculty that were possessed by his father. He can neither read nor write. From him I have obtained some of the earliest melodies and most archaic forms of ballads. Indeed the majority of his airs are in the old church modes, and generally end on the dominant. At one time his master sent him to Lydford on the edge of Dartmoor, to look after a farm he had bought. Whilst there, Parsons went every pay-day to a little moorland tavern, where the miners met to drink, and there he invariably got his 'entertainment' for his singing. 'I'd been zinging there,' said he, 'one evening till I got a bit fresh, and I thought 'twere time for me to be off. So I stood up to go, and then one chap, he said to me, "Got to the end o' your zongs, old man?" "Not I," said I, "not by a long ways; but I reckon it be time for me to be going." "Looky here, Jim," said he. "I'll give you a quart of ale for every fresh song you sing us to-night." Well, your honour, I sat down again, and I zinged on – I zinged sixteen fresh songs, and that chap had to pay for sixteen quarts.'

'Pints, surely,' I said.

'No, zur!' bridling up. 'No, zur – not pints, good English quarts. And then – I hadn't come to the end o' my zongs, only I were that fuddled, I couldn't remember no more.'

S. BARING GOULD

172

. . . there would be calls for old David's 'Outlandish Knight'; not because they wanted particularly to hear it – indeed, they had heard it so often they all knew it by heart – but because, as they said, 'Poor old feller be eighty-three. Let 'un sing while he can.'

So David would have his turn. He only knew the one ballad, and that, he said, his grandfather had sung, and had said that he had heard his own grandfather sing it. Probably a long chain of grandfathers had sung it; but David was fated to be the last of them. It was out of date, even then, and only tolerated on account of his age.

*

. . . As this last song was piped out in the aged voice, women at their cottage doors on summer evenings would say: 'They'll soon be out now. Poor old Dave's just singing his "Outlandish Knight".'

FLORA THOMPSON

The Ballad-Singer

Sing, Ballad-singer, raise a hearty tune;
    Make me forget that there was ever a one
I walked with in the meek light of the moon
        When the day's work was done.

Rhyme, Ballad-rhymer, start a country song;
Make me forget that she whom I loved well
Swore she would love me dearly, love me long,
        Then – what I cannot tell!

Sing, Ballad-singer, from your little book;
Make me forget those heart-breaks, achings, fears;
Make me forget her name, her sweet sweet look –
        Make me forget her tears.

THOMAS HARDY

Turnit Hoeing

Oh! I be a turnit hoer, from Zummerzetshire I came.
    My parents is hard working volks, Giles Webster be my
name.
'Twas on a zummer's mornin', e'en at the break of day,
When I took my hoe and off did go zum fifty miles away.

And zum delights in haymakin' and a vew be vond of mowin',
But of all the jobs that I like best, gi'e ae the turnit hoeing.
For the vlies, the vlies, the vlies be on the turnit,
And 'tis all no use for ae to try to keep them off the turnits.

O I be a tidy sort of chap and soon got I a place.
I went to work like any Turk and I took it by the piece;
And so I hoed on cheerfully and good Varmer Glower,
Who vowed and swore and said I wore a ripping turnit hoer.
And zum delights, etc.

In winter I drives oxen about the vields a-ploughin',
To keep the vurrow straight and clear all ready for turnit
    zowin'.
And when the vrost bars up the wheels, out on the land we're
    goin',
For without manure 'tis zertain zure, no turnits won't be
    growin'.
And zum delights, etc.

In on work about the varm yard until time brings me mowin',
For I like none of it half so well as I do my turnit hoein'.
And when the harvest now begins and the nut brown ale
    a-vlowin',
So I merely bids them all goodbye and I'm off to turnit hoein'.
And zum delights, etc.

TRADITIONAL

THE turnips, upon this farm, are by no means good; but I was in some measure compensated for the bad turnips by the sight of the duke's turnip-hoers, about a dozen females, amongst whom there were several very pretty girls, and they were as merry as larks. There had been a shower that had brought them into a sort of huddle on the roadside. When I came up to them, they all fixed their eyes upon me, and upon my smiling, they bursted out into laughter. I observed to them that the Duke of Buckingham was a very happy man to have such turnip-hoers, and really they seemed happier and better off than any work-people that I saw in the fields all the way from London to this spot. It is curious enough, but I have always observed that the women along this part of the country are usually tall. These girls were all tall, straight, fair, round-faced, excellent complexion, and uncommonly gay.

WILLIAM COBBETT

BACK through Upper Poppleton: and behind one of the farms in the village, pumping water in the yard, appeared a creature worth seeing. A farm servant girl really worthy of the name: tall & strong as a man – short thick neck and square massive shoulders – square broad back, straight from shoulder to hip with no waist to weaken it – stout, solid legs, & arms as thick as legs, bare and muscular throughout . . .

A. J. MUNBY

Now was the autumn come, and ploughers went forth to
  their ploughing;
    After the harvest was done, after the stubble was glean'd;
Ploughing the cornlands in, and turning up some of the
    fallows;
    Getting all ready to sow crops for the incoming year.
Oh, how delightful to see the exquisite sweep of the furrows
    Climbing in regular lines over the side of the hill!
Stretching in beautiful curves, as it seems at a distance, but
    really
    Straight as the strings of a harp; ranged in great octaves, like
      them.
For you shall see, in the sun, all purple and steely and shining,
    Ranges of long bright lines, all of them strictly alike;
But, at the end of each range, at equal intervals always,
    Comes a great deep bass line, carved like a trench – as it is.
Masterly art, in its way, and noble, the art of the ploughman!
    Well might our Dorothy feel proud of its 'glory and joy!'
For she was ploughing too; in the cool sweet air of October
    She too was out with the morn, scoring the slopes of the hill.
Under a hedge by the wood stood her plough, with its yoketree
    of scarlet –
    Symbol of all good work – waiting till Dolly should come;
Till she had harness'd the team, and with Billy the boy to
    attend her,
    Rode on the foremost horse, fresh for her labour of love.
For 'twas a labour of love, whereby she was earning her living:
    What can be better than that, either for woman or man?
Always to feel that your work is a thing that you know and are
    fit for,

Always to love it, and feel 'Yes, I am doing it well'!
That was what Dorothy felt, though she couldn't have told you
    her feelings,
    While she strode over the field after her horses, at plough;
Driving her furrows so straight, and trenching them round at
    the hedgerows,
    Guiding the stilts with a grasp skilful and strong as a man's.

A. J. MUNBY

178

A few women still did field work, not with the men, or even in
the same field as a rule, but at their own special tasks,
weeding and hoeing, picking up stones, and topping and tailing
turnips and mangel; or, in wet weather, mending sacks in a
barn. Formerly, it was said, there had been a large gang of field
women, lawless, slatternly creatures, some of whom had
thought nothing of having four or five children out of wedlock.
Their day was over; but the reputation they had left behind
them had given most country-women a distaste for 'goin'
afield'. In the 'eighties about half a dozen of the hamlet women
did field work, most of them being respectable middle-aged
women who, having got their families off hand, had spare time,
a liking for an open-air life, and a longing for a few shillings a
week they could call their own.

Their hours, arranged that they might do their housework
before they left home in the morning and cook their husband's
meal after they returned, were from ten to four, with an hour off
for dinner. Their wage was four shillings a week. They worked
in sunbonnets, hobnailed boots and men's coats, with coarse
aprons of sacking enveloping the lower part of their bodies.

One, a Mrs Spicer, was a pioneer in the wearing of trousers; she sported a pair of her husband's corduroys. The others compromised with ends of old trouser legs worn as gaiters. Strong, healthy, weather-beaten, hard as nails, they worked through all but the very worst weathers and declared they would go 'stark, staring mad' if they had to be shut up in a house all day.

FLORA THOMPSON

179

When a lot of women get together it's the pleasantest, for then there's company; but often we work alone – yesterday I was in this field alone, hoeing, from eight till five, all day.

SURREY WOMAN

180

THEN the gang system was in full force when I was a young man, and indeed right on into the sixties, though it was then beginning to die out. I have always been opposed to this form of labour organization. There were private gangs and public ones; small ones and large ones; fixed ones and wandering ones. Sometimes the gang would consist of one man and three or four children working under him; they would go turnip-singling and bean-dropping. Sometimes there would be a mixed gang of men and women weeding and picking 'twitch'; some would consist of women only. The potato gangs would be among the largest. You would see a line of women and children of all ages placed along a furrow at irregular distances; the piece allotted to each would vary a little and was called a 'stint', and all the potatoes in that furrow would have to be picked up before the plough came down the next one. Behind the line would be two or three carts, and the men with them would empty the baskets in. Such a gang would frequently number as many as seventy, and there would be a man walking up and down behind them superintending. Generally he was a rough bullying fellow, who could bluster and swear and threaten and knock the youngsters about and browbeat the women, but who was no-thing of a workman himself. Pea-picking gangs were generally very large, consisting of four and five hundred women and children. The language the women, and the children too, would use was beyond belief. Women who could get no decent indoor work, or who were rough and coarse and bold, would take to gang work, and instead of considering the poor little children by the side of them, these unnatural women have been known to teach the children vile language, and to encourage them in wickedness. There was no limit as to age, and I have seen little mites of things in potato fields who were hardly old enough to walk; and I have seen poor little toddlers set to turnip-singling when they should have been indoors with their mother.

JOSEPH ARCH

We Field-Women

How it rained
When we worked at Flintcomb-Ash,
And could not stand upon the hill
Trimming swedes for the slicing-mill.
The wet washed through us – plash, plash, plash:
    How it rained!

How it snowed
When we crossed from Flintcomb-Ash
To the Great Barn for drawing reed,
Since we could nowise chop a swede. –
Flakes in each doorway and casement-sash:
    How it snowed!

How it shone
When we went from Flintcomb-Ash
To start at dairywork once more
In the laughing meads, with cows three-score,
And pails, and songs, and love – too rash:
    How it shone!

THOMAS HARDY

182

Tess was afield. The dry winter wind still blew, but a screen
of thatched hurdles erected in the eye of the blast kept its
force away from her. On the sheltered side was a turnip-slicing

machine, whose bright blue hue of new paint seemed almost vocal in the otherwise subdued scene. Opposite its front was a long mound or 'grave', in which the roots had been preserved since early winter. Tess was standing at the uncovered end, chopping off with a bill-hook the fibres and earth from each root, and throwing it after the operation into the slicer. A man was turning the handle of the machine, and from its trough came the newly-cut swedes, the fresh smell of whose yellow chips was accompanied by the sounds of the snuffling wind, the smart swish of the slicing-blades, and the choppings of the hook in Tess's leather-gloved hand.

The wide acreage of blank agricultural brownness, apparent where the swedes had been pulled, was beginning to be striped in wales of darker brown, gradually broadening to ribands. Along the edge of each of these something crept upon ten legs, moving without haste and without rest up and down the whole length of the field; it was two horses and a man, the plough going between them, turning up the cleared ground for a spring sowing.

THOMAS HARDY

183

A dealer in agricultural machinery took a beet-cutter to demonstrate to a farmer. The farmer called one of his men and said: 'Here, George, you have a go at it. Tell me what you think on it.' An old worker, after giving the machine a jaundiced look, turned the handle and tried it with a few roots. Asked what he thought of it he said with conviction: 'It's some stiff, maaster. It whoolly sticks when you turn thet wheel: I fare to think it wants greasin'.' 'Send for Copping [the dealer]; he's just across the field a-looking at that harrow,' said the farmer. The verdict *It wants greasin'* was repeated to the dealer; but as he was a Suffolk man himself he summed up the situation in a moment. So as soon as the farmer's back was turned he slipped a shilling into the old boy's palm – 'Six pints o' beer at that time o' day' – and said to him: 'Just yew have a go at it now, bo'.' On being asked the second time by the farmer how the machine worked, the old worker said: 'It be whoolly fine now, maaster. It dew go like a rick on fire.'

GEORGE EWART EVANS

184

THE hedger soakd wi the dull weather chops
   On at his toils which scarcly keeps him warm
And every stroke he takes large swarms of drops
Patter about him like an april storm
The sticking dame wi cloak upon her arm
To guard against a storm walks the wet leas
Of willow groves or hedges round the farm
Picking up aught her splashy wanderings sees
Dead sticks the sudden winds have shook from off the trees

JOHN CLARE

Those dark nights were detested by the farm hands, the wind was like a carving-knife and it cut their hands and cheeks till they bled. They wrapped mufflers round their necks when they crossed the fields, and Joshua wore mittens so that his fingers were free, but they were frozen like boards, and caked with ice.

But wall-mending, milking, cattle-feeding, and watering had to go on, the cow-houses and stables were cleaned, the hens, calves, pigs, and sheep had to be fed. Turnips must be chopped, and slices of dry clean hay cut as neatly from the stack as a slice of bread from the loaf, with no slattering or waste.

Tom cut the hay, for Dan was a slatterer and Joshua's head could not stand the height of the ladder, nor was his hand steady enough to hold the cutting-knife. So Tom cut and Dan trussed the hay and carried it to the barns ready for foddering, a walking haystack as he staggered across the snowy field with only his two legs showing.

ALISON UTTLEY

186

Winter Fields

O for a pleasant book to cheat the sway
　Of winter – where rich mirth with hearty laugh
Listens and rubs his legs on corner seat
For fields are mire and sludge – and badly off
Are those who on their pudgy paths delay
There striding shepherd seeking driest way

Fearing nights wetshod feet and hacking cough
That keeps him waken till the peep of day
Goes shouldering onward and with ready hook
Progs oft to ford the sloughs that nearly meet
Accross the lands – croodling and thin to view
His loath dog follows – stops and quakes and looks
For better roads – till whistled to pursue
Then on with frequent jump he hirkles through

JOHN CLARE

187

I usd to spend many of my winter nights & Sabbath leisure when I grew up in the world at a neighbours house of the name of Billings   it was a sort of meeting-house for the young fellows of the town where they used to join for ale & tobacco & sing & drink the night away. The occupiers were two bachelors & the cottage was called 'Bachelors Hall'   it is an old ruinous hut & has needed repairs ever since I knew it for they neither mend up the walls nor thatch the roof being negligent men but quiet & inoffensive neighbours   I still frequent their house it has more the appearance of a deserted hermitage then an inhabited dwelling   I have sat talking of witch & ghost stories over our cups on winter nights till I felt fearful of going home   John Billings the elder had a very haunted mind for such things & had scarce been out on a journey with the night without seeing a gost will O whisp or some such shadowy mystery & such reccolections of midnight wanderings furnished him with storys for a whole winters fireside

JOHN CLARE

THERE were other shadows than those of chasing clouds and wheeling bird flocks over those fields. Ghost stories and stories of witchcraft lingered and were half believed. No one cared to go after dark to the cross roads where Dickie Bracknell, the suicide, was buried with a stake through his entrails, or to approach the barn out in the fields where he had hung himself some time at the beginning of the century. Bobbing lights were said to have been seen and gurgling sounds heard there.

Far out in the fields by the side of a wood was a pool which was said to be bottomless and haunted by a monster. No one could say exactly what the monster was like, for no one living had seen it, but the general idea was that it resembled a large newt, perhaps as big as a bullock. Among the children this pool was known as 'the beast's pond' and none of them ever went near it. Few people went that way, for the pond was cut off from the fields by a piece of uncultivated waste, and there was no path anywhere near it. Some fathers and mothers did not believe there was a pond there. It was just a silly old tale, they said, that folks used at one time to frighten themselves with. But there was a pond, for, towards the end of their schooldays, Edmund and Laura plodded over several ploughed fields and scrambled through as many hedges and pushed their way through a waste of dried thistles and ragwort and stood at last by a dark, still, tree-shadowed pool. No monster was there, only dark water, dark trees and a darkening sky and a silence so deep they could hear their own hearts pounding.

FLORA THOMPSON

A T Bradwell, in the Peak of Derbyshire, once lived a man known as Master John, who was reported to be a wise man, and whose advice was sought by all the people in the village. It is said that the ghost of a child who had been murdered in the village could not be appeased, and so the aid of Master John was invoked. Master John pronounced the words 'In the name of the Father, Son, and Holy Ghost, why troublest thou me' and turned the ghost of the child into a large fish. This fish used to appear, it is said, at a place called the Lum Mouth, and also at Lumley Pool, in Bradwell, on Christmas Day to people who fetched water from the wells there. When anybody saw the ghost in the form of a fish he would run away, screaming 'the fish, the fish'.

S. O. ADDY

190

A FTER breakfast I helped the cowman to feed the stock, staggering along under heavy skeps of meal and turnips to some dozen fat bullocks. I was too small to keep out of the muck, and waded through slop and cow-muck until I became absolutely lost. My breeches became so caked in pig-swill, calf-porridge, and meal I believe they could have stood upright without me inside them. My hands, by the same process, aided by the raw winds, became so swollen and cracked it was purgatory to wash them. And often I didn't. There was no one interested in whether I washed them or not, and so I degenerated into a 'reg'lar grub-etten little yarker', who cried and grinned, trying to force stiff, hard boots over broken chilblains. I must have looked unkempt and forlorn, but I was perfectly happy. I was too busy to be otherwise, and I always maintain that to be perfectly happy a person should get busy and interested in something.

FRED KITCHEN

The Honest Ploughman, or Ninety Years Ago

C OME all you jolly husbandmen, and listen to my song,
I'll relate the life of a ploughman, and not detain you
long.
My father was a farmer, who banished grief and woe,
My mother was a dairy maid – that's ninety years ago.

My father had a little farm, a harrow and a plough,
My mother had some pigs and fowls, a pony and a cow,
They didn't hire a servant, but they both their work did do,
As I have heard my parents say, just ninety years ago.

The rent that time was not so high by far, as I will pen,
For now one family's nearly twice as big as then were ten.
When I was born, my father used to harrow, plough and sow,
I think I've heard my mother say, 'twas ninety years ago.

To drive the plough my father did a boy engage,
Until that I had just arrived to seven years of age,
So then he did no servant want, my mother milk'd the cow,
And with the lark, I rose each morn, to go and drive the
  plough.

The farmers' wives in every way themselves the cows did milk,
They did not wear the dandy veils, and gowns made out of silk,
They did not ride blood horses, like the farmers' wives do now,
The daughters went a milking and the sons went to the plough.

When I was fifteen years of age, I used to thrash and sow,
Harrowed, ploughed, and in harvest time I used to reap and
  mow,
When I was twenty years of age, I could manage well the farm,
Could hedge and ditch, or plough, and sow, or thrash within
  the barn.

At length when I was twenty-five I took myself a wife,
Compelled to leave my father's house as I had changed my life,
The younger children, in my place, my father's work would do,
Then daily, as an husbandman, to labour I did go.

My wife and me, though very poor, could keep a pig and cow,
She could sit and spin and knit, and I the land could plough.
There nothing was upon a farm, at all, but I could do,
I find things very different now, – that's many years ago.

We lived along contented, and banished pain and grief,
We had not occasion then to ask for parish relief.
But now my hairs are grown quite grey, I cannot well engage,
To work as I had used to do, I'm ninety years of age.

But now that I am feeble grown, and poverty do feel,
If, for relief I go, they shove me into a Whig Bastile,
Where I may hang my hoary head, and pine in grief and woe,
My father did not see the like, just ninety years ago.

When a man has laboured all his life to do his country good,
He's respected just as much when old, as a donkey in a wood,
His days are gone and past, and he may weep in grief and woe,
The times are very different now to ninety years ago.

Now I am ninety years of age, if for relief I do apply,
I must go into a Whig Bastile to end my days and die,
I can no longer labour, as I no longer have,
Then, at the last, just like a dog, they lay me in my grave.

TRADITIONAL

192

IN truth, to whatever extent it may be brightened and
rendered habitable, one cannot pretend that a workhouse is
a cheerful place. The poor girls, with their illegitimate children
creeping, dirty-faced, across the floor of brick; the old, old
women lying in bed too feeble to move, or crouching round the
fire in their mob-caps, some of them stern-faced with much
gazing down the dim vista of the past, peopled for them with
dead, with much brooding on the present and the lot which it
has brought them; others vacuous and smiling – 'a little gone,'
the master whispers; others quite childish and full of com-
plaints, all of these are no more cheerful to look on than is the
dull appropriate light of this December afternoon. The old men,
too, their hands knobbed and knotted with decades of hard

work, their backs bent, their faces often almost grotesque, like those caricatures of humanity we see carved upon the handle of a stick, come here at last in reward of their labours – well, as the French writer says, '*cela donne furieusement à penser.*' It is not the place that is so melancholy, it is this poignant example of the sad end of life and all its toilings; it is the forlorn, half-dazed aspect of these battered human hulks who once were young, and strong, and comely.

RIDER HAGGARD

193

IN this parish dwells a vacuous but amiable old fellow called Turk Taylor, who has no belongings and picks up a living heaven knows how, for beyond a parish cottage which he occupies, and some small allowance from the rates, supplemented by an occasional job of pig-herding, he has no visible means of subsistence. Five or six years ago, in the course of a very hard winter, I heard that poor Turk Taylor had been found lying on the floor of his cottage at death's door from cold and starvation. He was attended to and his wants relieved, and afterwards an attempt was made to remove him to the workhouse. If I remember rightly the relieving officer actually came to fetch him, but the poor old man, getting wind of his designs, hid himself in a ditch until that official had departed, with the result that he still continues his free but precarious existence.

RIDER HAGGARD

ONE night when I called to see him, coming home from work, he burst into tears. 'Tha be gwoin' to take ma awoy, an I dwun want ta go,' he cried. I tried to comfort him, as well as I was able, but all to no purpose; he was beside himself with grief. And was it any wonder? Would *you* like to have gone, if *you* had been in his place? After living within those old walls, hallowed with memories of his mother and dad, his childhood and many things beside, for nearly eighty years, working and slaving, and sweating and stinting, for what? for what? But I have told you already. Of course he did not want to go; and quite right too. It was natural and manly, honest and brave; it is only the coward that thinks otherwise; and the spirit should be commended, not blamed and stifled down, and quenched out of existence. Several times the officers called and asked him if he would go to the 'house', but each time he answered defiantly, 'No, I wunt.' The old man shrank into the bed-clothes, and peered out at them over the top of the sheet. 'I'd soonder starve, an' die in mi bed fust, than go to that place,' he protested. Then the officers went away. The next day a conveyance stopped before the cottage, in came the officer again, and two men to carry him off. At first the old man wept like a child, then bawled and shouted at the interlopers: 'Lave ma alwun.' 'I wunt go.' 'Let ma die in mi bed.' 'Get a hatchet an chop mi 'ed off'; but all to no purpose. They dragged him out of bed, pulled a pair of woollen stockings on his shrunk shanks, clapped a blanket and an old coat around him, hauled him out of the cottage, slipped him in the conveyance, banged the door, and drove off as hard as they were able.

He did not live many weeks at the workhouse.

ALFRED WILLIAMS

WHEN once an aged man gives up, it seems strange at first that he should be so utterly helpless. In the infirmary the real benefit of the workhouse reached him. The food, the little luxuries, the attention were far superior to anything he could possibly have had at home. But still it was not home. The windows did not permit him from his bed to see the leafless trees or the dark woods and distant hills. Left to himself, it is certain that of choice he would have crawled under a rick, or into a hedge, if he could not have reached his cottage.

The end came very slowly; he ceased to exist by imperceptible degrees, like an oak-tree. He remained for days in a semi-conscious state, neither moving nor speaking. It happened at last. In the grey of the winter dawn, as the stars paled and the whitened grass was stiff with hoar frost, and the rime coated every branch of the tall elms, as the milker came from the pen and the young ploughboy whistled down the road to his work, the spirit of the aged man departed.

RICHARD JEFFERIES

196

The Bedridden Peasant

To an Unknowing God

MUCH wonder I – here long low-laid –
    That this dead wall should be
Betwixt the Maker and the made,
    Between Thyself and me!

For, say one puts a child to nurse,
   He eyes it now and then
To know if better it is, or worse,
   And if it mourn, and when.

But Thou, Lord, giv'st us men our day
   In helpless bondage thus
To Time and Chance, and seem'st straightway
   To think no more of us!

That some disaster cleft Thy scheme
   And tore us wide apart,
So that no cry can cross, I deem;
   For Thou art mild of heart,

And wouldst not shape and shut us in
   Where voice can not be heard:
Plainly Thou meant'st that we should win
   Thy succour by a word.

Might but Thy sense flash down the skies
   Like man's from clime to clime,
Thou wouldst not let me agonize
   Through my remaining time;

But, seeing how much Thy creatures bear –
   Lame, starved, or maimed, or blind –
Wouldst heal the ills with quickest care
   Of me and all my kind.

Then, since Thou mak'st not these things be,
   But these things dost not know,
I'll praise Thee as were shown to me
   The mercies Thou wouldst show!

THOMAS HARDY

THE old road-mender is nearly eighty now. He is very small in stature, but just over four feet high. His features are small and regular; he is fine-looking – well-shaped nose, taper forehead, blue eyes, grey hair, moustache, and side whiskers. His shoulders are bent a little – they have borne many a heavy sack of corn from the thresher to the granary – and he is half a cripple. His left leg is in the shape of a bow; in walking he swings this round somewhat, and especially if he has imbibed a glass or two of fourpenny; then he will have great difficulty in maintaining a dignified gait as he totters off, stick in hand, and basket on arm, down the road to his cottage. The old man is his own master, servant, and everything combined. He lights his fires, prepares his food, washes up and cleans the house, makes his own bed – is cook, chamber-maid, and scullery-maid together. Often in the summer months he rises at four, and lights the fire to cook the sweet green peas and young 'taters'. After that he potters about till seven or eight, then goes to view his vegetable crops in the allotment; he has acquired great local fame as an horticulturist, and he usually tops the list for fine produce in the garden. After due inspection of the onion-bed and potato-patch, and comparing them with others in the field, he may visit the inn for a morning glass and a chat with the landlord; then, if it is fine, he lies down in the shade of the withy-tree, or elder-boughs, till dinner-time, and very often all day, then loads himself with produce, and goes home to his cottage again. Here he cooks for tea or supper, eats the meal in silence, and retires about eight. The great problems of the day and hour do not disturb his manner of living; in spite of his losses and misfortunes he is happy and satisfied.

ALFRED WILLIAMS

The Old Farm Labourer

I saw the load birth laid on him.
    The common burden of the poor
Long dark unlettered labour dim,
Old age and death and nothing more.

I saw him stretched on his death bed.
I did not say in heaven all's healed.
He lifted up his heavy head
And gazed and gazed across a field.

He moved aside his cotton sheet
His thin legs hung o'er the mattress edge,
He stood up on unsteady feet
And keenly eyed a ragged hedge.

He curved his right hand to a crook
The zest of labour lit his eye.
He said if I could hold a hook
I'd plash that hedge before I die.

ANON.

Holly and Ivy

My father left me a good acre of land –
   Sing holly, sing ivy;
My father left me a good acre of land,
And a bunch of green holly and ivy.

I ploughed it up with a team of rats –
   Sing holly, sing ivy;
I ploughed it up with a team of rats,
And a bunch of green holly and ivy.

I harrowed it with a small-toothed comb –
   Sing holly, sing ivy;
I harrowed it with a small-toothed comb,
And a bunch of green holly and ivy.

I sowed some pepper-corns and they came up –
   Sing holly, sing ivy;
I sowed some peppercorns and they came up,
And a bunch of green holly and ivy.

I reaped it with my little penknife –
   Sing holly, sing ivy;
I reaped it with my little penknife,
And a bunch of green holly and ivy.

I thrashed it with a little beanstalk –
   Sing holly, sing ivy;
I thrashed it with a little beanstalk,
And a bunch of green holly and ivy.

I winnowed it with the tail of my shirt –
    Sing holly, sing ivy;
I winnowed it with the tail of my shirt,
And a bunch of green holly and ivy.

I sent it to market with a team of rats –
    Sing holly, sing ivy;
I sent it to market with a team of rats,
And a bunch of green holly and ivy.

The rats they all came galloping back –
    Sing holly, sing ivy;
The rats they all came galloping back,
And a bunch of green holly and ivy.

TRADITIONAL

200

CHRISTMASS is come and every hearth
    Makes room to give him welcome now
Een want will dry its tears in mirth
And crown him wi a holly bough
Tho tramping neath a winters sky
Oer snow track paths and ryhmey stiles
The huswife sets her spining bye
And bids him welcome wi her smiles

*

The shepherd now no more afraid
Since custom doth the chance bestow
Starts up to kiss the giggling maid
Beneath the branch of mizzletoe
That neath each cottage beam is seen
Wi pearl-like-berrys shining gay
The shadow still of what hath been
Which fashion yearly fades away

And singers too a merry throng
At early morn wi simple skill
Yet imitate the angels song
And chant their christmass ditty still
And mid the storm that dies and swells
By fits – in humings softly steals
The music of the village bells
Ringing round their merry peals

And when its past a merry crew
Bedeckt in masks and ribbons gay
The 'Morrice danse' their sports renew
And act their winter evening play
The clown-turnd-kings for penny praise
Storm wi the actors strut and swell
And harlequin a laugh to raise
Wears his hump back and tinkling bell

And oft for pence and spicy ale
Wi winter nosgays pind before
The wassail singer tells her tale
And drawls her christmass carrols oer

The prentice boy wi ruddy face
And rŷhme bepowderd dancing locks
From door to door wi happy pace
Runs round to claim his 'christmass box'

JOHN CLARE

201

W HEN, from the comparative quiet within, the mummers judged that the dancers had taken their seats, Father Christmas advanced, lifted the latch, and put his head inside the door.

'Ah, the mummers, the mummers!' cried several guests at once. 'Clear a space for the mummers.'

Hump-backed Father Christmas then made a complete entry, swinging his huge club, and in a general way clearing the stage for the actors proper, while he informed the company in smart verse that he was come, welcome or welcome not; concluding his speech with

'Make room, make room, my gallant boys,
    And give us space to rhyme;
We've come to show Saint George's play,
    Upon this Christmas time.'

THOMAS HARDY

Thames Head Wassailers' Song

Wassail, wassail, all over the town,
Our toast is white and our ale is brown,
Our bowl it is made of a maplin tree,
And so is good beer of the best barley.

Here's to the ox, and to his long horn;
May God send our maester a good crap o' corn!
A good crap o' corn, and another o' hay,
To pass the cold wintry winds away.

Here's to the ox, and to his right ear;
May God send our maester a happy New Year!
A happy New Year, as we all may see,
With our wassailing bowl we will drink unto thee.

Here's to old Jerry, and to her right eye;
May God send our mistress a good Christmas pie!
A good Christmas pie, as we all may see,
And a wassailing bowl we will drink unto thee.

Here's to old Boxer, and to his long tail;
I hope that our maester'll hae n'er a 'oss vail!
N'er a 'oss vail, as we all may see,
And a wassailing bowl we will drink unto thee.

Come, pretty maidens – I suppose there are some!
Never let us poor young men stand on the cold stone;
The stones they are cold, and our shoes they are thin,
The fairest maid in the house let us come in!
Let us come in, and see how you do.

Maid: Yes, if you will, and welcome, too!

Here's to the maid, and the rosemary tree,
The ribbons are wanted, and that you can see;
The ribbons are wanted, and that you can see,
With our wassailing bowl we will drink unto thee.

Now, boteler, come, fill us a bowl o' the best,
And we hope that thy sowl in heaven may rest;
But if you do bring us a bowl o' the small,
Then down shall go boteler, bowl and all,
Bowl and all, bowl and all;
Then down shall go boteler, bowl and all.

Now, master and mistress, if you are within,
Send down some of your merry, merry men,
That we may eat and drink before the clock strikes ten,
    Our jolly wassail;
When joy comes unto our jolly wassail.

TRADITIONAL

203

Room for a Little One

BRIDGET were the little maid at the big inn where all they travellers comes and she were on her two little feet from daybreak till the chime hours, a-running up and down with all she had to do in the kitchens, and as if that weren't enough she had to be off and gather wood from the Selwood Forest and see and bring it in for firing – great loads too – but they did think to give she a little nirrip so as she could bring two loads to the once back home. And when all t'other Christian souls was warm and snoring hours since she just about finished the washing and cleaning and mending up the fires, and then she run out shivering in her bare feet to the nirrip's stable to get warm again, crowded up against the little rough coat. 'Twas a very little nirrip and a very little stable – just a old shed with old thatch the stars shined down through, and room for a little one – but they both of they made it two and contrived to sleep sound till cockcrow.

There come one bitter cold night, snow and frost, and the inn was full up to the roof-tree, with stables and bartons full of beasts too.

Bridget and the nirrip come back numb to the bone and that loaded you couldn't see nothing under the firing but their feet, and they was like blue ice-blocks; and there in the yard were a bone-weary, clarty old hungry plough-ox, left without a mouthful of hay or shelter, and freezing to death he was, and they both couldn't have that.

'I got a stable,' says the nirrip.

'And there's be a bit of hay too,' says Bridget.

''Tis ours,' they said, 'but there's room for a little one.'

The old ox took a look at it.

One great star were a-shining down into the yard and into thic stable too and somehow it did have a look big enough for a mortal freezing old ox.

And somehow it were.

And somehow there were quite a goodish bit of hay inside as well.

So Bridget let the nirrip creep in too – and away with her to make up the fires. She thaw her feet a bit that way and then, would you believe it, they said they'd need more wood.

Back to the girt, black forest she and the poor little nirrip must trudge again in all the bitter wind and frost, so her went to tell the creature and her nearly cried when her did. The little small thing were so stiff and numbed as she were.

''Twill be wicked black dark,' says Bridget. 'Oh, I be that a-feared to go.'

'I've a cross on my back,' says the nirrip speaking up brave. 'And that there star a-shining above will show the way,' says the old ox comforting. 'I'll a-come back too if you do like, then us'll only be needing one girt big load.' So, tired to death as they all was, they goes to the forest.

Bridget she had a slice of stale bread from the pig bucket, and the nirrip and the old ox still chewed a bit of hay – 'twasn't much but something to keep 'en from starving, and they got their load.

Then they all seed somebody under the starlight. A man and a woman 'twas, and they were just about so tired as the three of them was. The man was a-helping the woman who couldn't hardly walk no more.

'She do need shelter,' said Bridget. 'And food and a bed – and there were no room in the inn.'

'There's my stable,' said the nirrip under her great load.

'And room for a little one,' said the ox all a-shiver as he staggered.

So the man he up and took the little nirrip's wood and the woman rode on a tired, careful little back.

Ever so careful nirrip were, and they all found they was going back to inn quite fast in the starlight.

Then Bridget she saw the man and woman go thankful into the little stable, and they beckon the nirrip and the ox inside too, then they all called out to Bridget standing in the snow and starshine all in her bare feet, 'There's room for a Little One!'

'I'll come, my dears, when I've a-done my work,' said Bridget, and away she went and dragged the wood to the hearth where the ox's master lay drink-taken and she washed and cleared up, and found a bit of clean bread and cheese.

She took that out along with her. She'd a notion they must be hungry in the stable – and the star shone bright as if it were dancing and Bridget's feet they danced too.

So out she run and the stable was all a-lit by the great star and God's dear Son was there too with the others and there was angels singing – the nirrip were a-singing too.

> I gave Him my manger all full of sweet hay;
> I knelt with the shepherds on Chrissimas Day.
> The Star it shone over – and loud I did bray.
> Gloria in excelsis!
> Christ the Lord is born!

RUTH TONGUE

204

PRISCILLA said, 'I have known old James Meredith 40 years and I have never known him far from the truth, and I said to him one day, "James, tell me the truth, did you ever see the oxen kneel on old Christmas Eve at the Weston?" And he said, "No, I never saw them kneel at the Weston but when I was at Hinton at Staunton-on-Wye I saw them. I was watching them on old Christmas Eve and at 12 o'clock the oxen that were standing knelt down upon their knees and those that were lying down rose up on their knees and there they stayed kneeling and moaning, the tears running down their faces."'

FRANCIS KILVERT

The Oxen

CHRISTMAS Eve, and twelve of the clock.
  'Now they are all on their knees,'
An elder said as we sat in a flock
  By the embers in hearthside ease.

We pictured the meek mild creatures where
  They dwelt in their strawy pen,
Nor did it occur to one of us there
  To doubt they were kneeling then.

So fair a fancy few would weave
  In these years! Yet, I feel,
If someone said on Christmas Eve,
  'Come; see the oxen kneel

'In the lonely barton by yonder coomb
  Our childhood used to know,'
I should go with him in the gloom,
  Hoping it might be so.

1915

THOMAS HARDY

Old Shepherd's Prayer

Up to the bed by the window, where I be lyin',
 Comes bells and bleat of the flock wi' they two children's
  clack.
Over, from under the eaves there's the starlings flyin',
And down in yard, fit to burst his chain, yapping out at Sue I
  do hear young Mac.

Turning around like a falled-over sack
I can see team ploughin' in Whithy-bush field and meal carts
  startin' up road to Church-Town;
Saturday arternoon the men goin' back
And the women from market, trapin' home over the down.

Heavenly Master, I wud like to wake to they same green places
Where I be know'd for breakin' dogs and follerin' sheep.
And if I may not walk in th' old ways and look on th' old faces
I wud sooner sleep.

CHARLOTTE MEW

207

Lob

At hawthorn-time in Wiltshire travelling
 In search of something chance would never bring,
An old man's face, by life and weather cut
And coloured, – rough, brown, sweet as any nut, –

A land face, sea-blue-eyed, – hung in my mind
When I had left him many a mile behind.
All he said was: 'Nobody can't stop 'ee. It's
A footpath, right enough. You see those bits
Of mounds – that's where they opened up the barrows
Sixty years since, while I was scaring sparrows.
They thought as there was something to find there,
But couldn't find it, by digging, anywhere.'

To turn back then and seek him, where was the use?
There were three Manningfords, – Abbots, Bohun, and Bruce:
And whether Alton, not Manningford, it was,
My memory could not decide, because
There was both Alton Barnes and Alton Priors.
All had their churches, graveyards, farms and byres,
Lurking to one side up the paths and lanes,
Seldom well seen except by aeroplanes;
And when bells rang, or pigs squealed, or cocks crowed,
Then only heard. Ages ago the road
Approached. The people stood and looked and turned.
Nor asked it to come nearer, nor yet learned
To move out there and dwell in all men's dust.
And yet withal they shot the weathercock, just
Because 'twas he crowed out of tune, they said:
So now the copper weathercock is dead.
If they had reaped their dandelions and sold
Them fairly, they could have afforded gold.

Many years passed, and I went back again
Among those villages, and looked for men
Who might have known my ancient. He himself
Had long been dead or laid upon the shelf,
I thought. One man I asked about him roared
At my description: ''Tis old Bottlesford

He means, Bill.' But another said: 'Of course,
It was Jack Button up at the White Horse.
He's dead, sir, these three years.' This lasted till
A girl proposed Walker of Walker's Hill,
'Old Adam Walker. Adam's Point you'll see
Marked on the maps.'

              'That was her roguery,'
The next man said. He was a squire's son
Who loved wild bird and beast, and dog and gun
For killing them. He had loved them from his birth,
One with another, as he loved the earth.
'The man may be like Button, or Walker, or
Like Bottlesford, that you want, but far more
He sounds like one I saw when I was a child.
I could almost swear to him. The man was wild
And wandered. His home was where he was free.
Everybody has met one such man as he.
Does he keep clear old paths that no one uses
But once a lifetime when he loves or muses?
He is English as this gate, these flowers, this mire.
And when at eight years old Lob-lie-by-the-fire
Came in my books, this was the man I saw.
He has been in England as long as dove and daw,
Calling the wild cherry tree the merry tree,
The rose campion Bridget-in-her-bravery;
And in a tender mood he, as I guess,
Christened one flower Love-in-idleness,
And while he walked from Exeter to Leeds
One April called all cuckoo-flowers Milkmaids.
From him old herbal Gerard learnt, as a boy,
To name wild clematis the Traveller's-joy.
Our blackbirds sang no English till his ear
Told him they called his Jan Toy 'Pretty dear'.

(She was Jan Toy the Lucky, who, having lost
A shilling, and found a penny loaf, rejoiced.)
For reasons of his own to him the wren
Is Jenny Pooter. Before all other men
'Twas he first called the Hog's Back the Hog's Back.
That Mother Dunch's Buttocks should not lack
Their name was his care. He too could explain
Totteridge and Totterdown and Juggler's Lane:
He knows, if anyone. Why Tumbling Bay,
Inland in Kent, is called so, he might say.

'But little he says compared with what he does.
If ever a sage troubles him he will buzz
Like a beehive to conclude the tedious fray:
And the sage, who knows all languages, runs away.
Yet Lob has thirteen hundred names for a fool,
And though he never could spare time for school
To unteach what the fox so well expressed,
On biting the cock's head off, – Quietness is best, –
He can talk quite as well as anyone
After his thinking is forgot and done.
He first of all told someone else's wife,
For a farthing she'd skin a flint and spoil a knife
Worth sixpence skinning it. She heard him speak:
'She had a face as long as a wet week'
Said he, telling the tale in after years.
With blue smock and with gold rings in his ears,
Sometimes he is a pedlar, not too poor
To keep his wit. This is tall Tom that bore
The logs in, and with Shakespeare in the hall
Once talked, when icicles hung by the wall.
As Herne the Hunter he has known hard times.
On sleepless nights he made up weather rhymes

Which others spoilt. And, Hob being then his name,
He kept the hog that thought the butcher came
To bring his breakfast. 'You thought wrong,' said Hob.
When there were kings in Kent this very Lob,
Whose sheep grew fat and he himself grew merry,
Wedded the king's daughter of Canterbury;
For he alone, unlike squire, lord, and king,
Watched a night by her without slumbering;
He kept both waking. When he was but a lad
He won a rich man's heiress, deaf, dumb, and sad,
By rousing her to laugh at him. He carried
His donkey on his back. So they were married.
And while he was a little cobbler's boy
He tricked the giant coming to destroy
Shrewsbury by flood. 'And how far is it yet?'
The giant asked in passing. 'I forget;
But see these shoes I've worn out on the road
And we're not there yet.' He emptied out his load
Of shoes for mending. The giant let fall from his spade
The earth for damming Severn, and thus made
The Wrekin hill; and little Ercall hill
Rose where the giant scraped his boots. While still
So young, our Jack was chief of Gotham's sages.
But long before he could have been wise, ages
Earlier than this, while he grew thick and strong
And ate his bacon, or, at times, sang a song
And merely smelt it, as Jack the giant-killer
He made a name. He too ground up the miller,
The Yorkshireman who ground men's bones for flour.

'Do you believe Jack dead before his hour?
Or that his name is Walker, or Bottlesford,
Or Button, a mere clown, or squire, or lord?

The man you saw, – Lob-lie-by-the-fire, Jack Cade,
Jack Smith, Jack Moon, poor Jack of every trade,
Young Jack, or old Jack, or Jack What-d'ye-call,
Jack-in-the-hedge, or Robin-run-by-the-wall,
Robin Hood, Ragged Robin, lazy Bob,
One of the lords of No Man's Land, good Lob, –
Although he was seen dying at Waterloo,
Hastings, Agincourt, and Sedgemoor too,
Lives yet. He never will admit he is dead
Till millers cease to grind men's bones for bread,
Not till our weathercock crows once again
And I remove my house out of the lane
On to the road.' With this he disappeared
In hazel and thorn tangled with old-man's-beard.
But one glimpse of his back, as there he stood,
Choosing his way, proved him of old Jack's blood,
Young Jack perhaps, and now a Wiltshireman
As he has oft been since his days began.

EDWARD THOMAS

208

T HE last party for the convalescents was a terrifically jolly
affair. They were to sail tomorrow and I prised Dick
Garland from a lonely corner behind a potted palm-plant and
found a window-seat in which he might once more sing to solace
our heartaches for a too distant Somerset. ''Tis a bit of old lost
song but there's withies in it,' he managed to say.

Langport Town or The Water Witch

The refrain sung by Richard Garland near Birmingham, Autumn 1917

By the beds of green withies a young man I espied,
Lamenting his true love, lamenting his bride.
All on a summer morning she went to Langport town,
But she never comed home again, she never comed home again,
She never comed home again, when the moon it went down.
Oh Ellum do grieve, and Oak he do hate,
But Willow, Willow, Willow,
Willow do walk if you travel late.

By the beds of green withies when morning did arise
He found his dear Nanny, all a-drownèd she lies.
All on a summer morning she went to Langport Town, etc.

'I have lost my dearest Nanny,' he sobbed and he cried
'Afloating down river, all a-drift on the tide,'
All on a summer morning she went to Langport Town, etc.

He only knew the chorus, but he sang and I sang too, very quietly, and then we were collected in for a rowdy sing-song and then the men had to go. The air was loaded with thanks and jokes, and as ever he was the last to go.

He turned shyly in the doorway and said, 'Well, goodnight all,' and went, and the shadow was over him as he did.

He was killed in France within the week.

Years later, I was sitting with a cheerful Exmoor farmhouse group all enjoying an evening's singing of songs – mine and theirs, old and new, but mostly the songs of tradition. A farmer uncle seated on the settle listened to them in silence and when at last we desisted for a moment from sheer exhaustion he rose and made a slow way to the door for his long moorland road homewards. In the doorway he paused in his going, 'My boy he knowed all they old songs – ah – and a good many more – *but he never come back*. Well – goodnight all.'

RUTH TONGUE

209

In Time of 'The Breaking of Nations'

I

Only a man harrowing clods
   In a slow silent walk
With an old horse that stumbles and nods
   Half asleep as they stalk.

II

Only thin smoke without flame
   From the heaps of couch-grass;
Yet this will go onward the same
   Though Dynasties pass.

III

Yonder a maid and her wight
   Come whispering by:
War's annals will cloud into night
   Ere their story die.

   1915

THOMAS HARDY

NOTES AND SOURCES

(Numbers quoted are extract numbers)

1. RUDYARD KIPLING, *Rewards and Fairies* (Macmillan, London, 1910).

2. EDWARD THOMAS, *Collected Poems* (Clarendon Press, Oxford, 1978).

3. RICHARD JEFFERIES, *The Toilers of the Field* (Longmans, Green & Co., London, 1892). This collection (reissued with an introduction by Victor E. Neuburg in 1981) appeared five years after Jefferies' death, and includes the letters to *The Times* which made his name, in which he blames the labourers themselves for their plight – 'It is the labourer himself who will not rise' – as well as some of the later essays in which Jefferies is much more sympathetic to the farmworkers' viewpoint. This extract is from the essay 'The Labourer's Daily Life'.

4. JOHN CLARE, *The Shepherd's Calendar*, ed. E. Robinson and G. Summerfield (Oxford University Press, London, 1964). The first – 1827 – edition of this poem, Clare's greatest work, was savagely edited and amended by his publisher John Taylor. This extract from 'January: A Winter's Day' was among the cuts. Clare's deliberate lack of punctuation is initially alarming, but presents surprisingly few problems in practice. Clare constantly identified nature with the poetic impulse, and the misspelling 'ryhme' for 'rime' introduces a cherishable ambiguity here.

5. ROBERT BLOOMFIELD, *The Farmer's Boy* (Vernon & Hood, London, 1800). Bloomfield was a shoemaker, who drew on his childhood memories for this long poem, which enjoyed great popularity. Later work rarely recaptured its freshness. He died in poverty in 1823. Clare revered him. A 'beetle' was a heavy mallet: hence the pub sign 'The Beetle and Wedge'.

6. FRANK PURSLOW, *Foggy Dew* (English Folk Dance and Song Society, London, 1974). Text from a broadside issued by Wright of Birmingham. None of the broadsides in the Bodleian has the last verse; they all have a third verse:

Brotherly love did then abound, oppression ne'er was heard,
But now the people are so poor they scarcely can get bread,
Which makes them wander up and down not knowing what to do;
Such times did not abound when my old hat was new.

7. FLORA THOMPSON, *Lark Rise to Candleford* (Oxford University Press, Oxford, 1945; Penguin, Harmondsworth, 1973). This lightly fictionalized autobiographical trilogy (first published as separate volumes, 1939, 1941, 1943) is one of the best depictions of late nineteenth-century village life, and one of the few from the female point of view. Its reputation for sentimentality is quite undeserved. Flora Thompson was born in 1876 at Juniper Hill on the Oxfordshire–Northamptonshire border, the 'Lark Rise' of the books.

8. EBENEZER ELLIOTT, *Poetical Works* (Henry S. King & Son, London, 1876). From 'The Splendid Village', first published 1833. Elliott was known as 'the Corn-Law Rhymer'.

9. JOHN CLARE, *Selected Poems and Prose*, ed. E. Robinson & G. Summerfield (Oxford University Press, London, 1966). Clare was born in 1793. His native village of Helpston in Northamptonshire was enclosed by Act of Parliament in 1809. The enclosure deeply saddened Clare, and provided him with an apt metaphor with which to explore and contrast the imaginative freedom of his childhood and the constricting limitation of his adult life. Today's historians are less inclined to blame enclosure alone for the reduced status of the nineteenth-century agricultural labourer than were those of a previous generation, but Clare is certainly an eloquent witness to the depth of feeling against it which others must have shared but been unable to express.

10. GEORGE BOURNE (GEORGE STURT), *Change in the Village* (Duckworth, London, 1912). The village is Bourne in Surrey.

11. THOMAS HOOD, *Complete Poetical Works*, ed. W. Jerrold (Oxford University Press, London, 1935). First published 1844.

12. B. S. ROWNTREE and M. KENDALL, *How the Labourer Lives* (Nelson, London, 1913); a sociological study comparable to M. Pember Reeves's *Round About a Pound a Week*. Mrs West lived in Oxfordshire.

13. ROWNTREE and KENDALL, *How the Labourer Lives* (see previous note). 'Sad cake' is unrisen; presumably using up some of that 21 lbs of flour.

245

14. ROWNTREE and KENDALL, *How the Labourer Lives* (see note 12). Mrs Bell lived in Berkshire.

15. ALEXANDER SOMERVILLE, *The Whistler at the Plough* (James Ainsworth, Manchester, 1852). A survey of agricultural labour originally undertaken for the Anti-Corn-Law League. Somerville wrote an interesting account of his own life, *The Autobiography of a Working Man* (1848). The conversation with the ploughboy took place 'on a large farm near Abingdon'.

16. M. K. ASHBY, *Joseph Ashby of Tysoe 1859–1919* (Cambridge University Press, Cambridge, 1961; reissued with an introduction by E. P. Thompson, 1974). M. K. Ashby's biography of her father is a magnificent example of scholarship deployed in the service of deep feeling, and deserves to be much more widely known. Tysoe is in South Warwickshire.

17. JEFFERIES, *The Toilers of the Field* (see note 3). An extract from Jefferies' first letter to *The Times* on the Wiltshire labourers, dated 12 November 1872.

18. GEORGE ELIOT, *Silas Marner* (William Blackwood & Sons, Edinburgh and London, 1861; Penguin, Harmondsworth, 1967).

19. THOMPSON, *Lark Rise to Candleford* (see note 7).

20. G. F. NORTHALL, *English Folk-Rhymes* (Kegan Paul, Trench, Trubner & Co., London, 1892).

21. ROY PALMER, *Everyman's Book of English Country Songs* (Dent, London, 1979). Communicated to Mr Palmer by Mr Maurice Ogg, Coleby, Lincs., who notes that various versions of the song are popular in the locality. 'Yowe' = ewe. One acre a day was the normal ploughing stint. Mr Palmer's book offers an excellent selection of country songs, with music, helpfully annotated.

22. THOMPSON, *Lark Rise to Candleford* (see note 7).

23. FRED HAMER, *Garners Gay* (English Folk Dance and Song Society, London, 1967). Collected from Frank Rowe of East Cornwall.

24. GERARD MANLEY HOPKINS, *Poems*, ed. R. Bridges, 2nd edition (Oxford University Press, London, 1930).

25. BLOOMFIELD, *The Farmer's Boy* (see note 5).

26. JOHN MASEFIELD, *Collected Poems* (Heinemann, London, 1923). From 'The Everlasting Mercy'. This is the moment of Saul Kane's conversion; I have

omitted some lines which refer to this, though the intensity of description retains the essential feeling.

27. PALMER, *English Country Songs* (see note 21). Reprinted from J. Broadwood, *Old English Songs*, 1843.

28. ALFRED WILLIAMS, *Folk-Songs of the Upper Thames* (Duckworth, London, 1923). Williams (1877–1930) was the last of a line of self-educated rural poets stretching from Stephen Duck (1705–56) through Bloomfield and Clare. He wrote an interesting autobiographical work, *Life in a Railway Factory* (1915). There is a biography by Leonard Clark, *Alfred Williams: His Life and Work* (1945) . 'Mornty' is glossed by him as 'Morn't'e = Good morning to ye'.

29. THOMAS HARDY, *Tess of the D'Urbervilles* (Penguin, Harmondsworth, 1978). First published 1891, referring to the 1860s and 1870s.

30. W. H. BARRETT and R. P. GARROD, *East Anglian Folklore and Other Tales* (Routledge & Kegan Paul, London, 1976). The quotation is from Mr Garrod's diary of his conversations with W. H. Barrett, whose expertise as a storyteller can be sampled also in *Tales from the Fens* (1963) and *More Tales from the Fens* (1964). He was born in 1891.

31. ISAAC MEAD, *The Life Story of an Essex Lad: Written by Himself* (A. Driver & Sons, Chelmsford, 1923). Mr Mead was born in 1859.

32. CLARE, *The Shepherd's Calendar*, 'May' (see note 4). 'Frail' is an alternative for 'flail'.

33. HAMER, *Garners Gay* (see note 23). Collected from William Bleasdale.

34. DOROTHY WORDSWORTH, *Journals*, ed. E. de Selincourt (Macmillan, London, 1941). Entry dated 16 April 1802.

35. THOMAS CARLYLE. Text from A. T. Quiller-Couch, *The Oxford Book of Victorian Verse* (Clarendon Press, Oxford, 1912). Alfred Williams collected an oral version of this from Mrs Mackie, Lechlade, and printed it in *Folk-Songs of the Upper Thames*, noting it as 'a superior piece, not heard out of North Wilts'. The text in *Fraser's Magazine III*, 1831, differs considerably.

36. CLARE, *The Shepherd's Calendar*, 'March' (see note 4).

37. NORTHALL, *English Folk-Rhymes* (see note 20).

38. WILLIAMS, *Folk-Songs of the Upper Thames* (see note 28).

39. GERTRUDE JEKYLL, *Old West Surrey* (Longmans, Green & Co., London, 1904). Among the many valuable illustrations to this book are a photograph of the anonymous author of this rough-verse autobiography – a ninety-year-old woman who lived near Godalming – and a reproduction of two pages of the manuscript. Though hard to follow, this document becomes easier to understand – as does Clare – when read for sound rather than spelling. 'DHUGED', for instance, is presumably 'dogged'; 'AT · TOME' is 'at home'. I take the eighth verse ('My mother was so kind') to be commending the mother for never wishing to roam gossiping, but preferring to stay at home with her children. The contrast between this woman's wish to express the meaning and shape of her life and her ability to do so tells its own story.

40. Royal Commission on the Employment of Children, Young Persons, and Women in Agriculture (Parliamentary Papers, 1867–8, vol. XVII). Irchester is in Northamptonshire.

41. JOSEPH ARCH, *Joseph Arch: the story of his life, told by himself*, ed. Countess of Warwick (Hutchinson, London, 1898). A key document of labour history. Arch was born in Barford, South Warwickshire in 1826. He formed the first National Agricultural Labourers' Union in 1872, and became an M.P. in 1885. He died at Barford in 1919. There is a good modern biography by Pamela Horn, *Joseph Arch* (1971). Howard Newby, in his challenging study of contemporary farmworkers, *The Deferential Worker* (1977), is contemptuously dismissive of Arch; a truer estimate of him may be found in E. W. Martin's statement (in *The Secret People: English Village Life after 1750* (1954)) that, 'There are old labourers still living whose roughened lips quiver at the mention of the name of "Joe Arch".'

42. SYBIL MARSHALL, *Fenland Chronicle* (Cambridge University Press, Cambridge, 1967). This book, though written in the first person as the memoirs of William Henry and Kate Mary Edwards, was put together by their daughter Sybil. This extract comes from Mrs Edwards' half of the book.

43. MARGARET LLEWELYN DAVIES (ed.), *Life as We Have Known It* (Hogarth Press, London, 1931). From Mrs Burrows, 'A Childhood in the Fens about 1850–60'. This book was a product of the Women's Co-operative Guild; it was reissued with an introduction by Anna Davin in 1977.

44. Royal Commission on Agriculture (1867–8) (see note 40). Ellen Brown came from Metheringham in Lincolnshire.

45. JEKYLL, *Old West Surrey* (see note 39).

46. AUGUSTUS JESSOPP, *Arcady: For Better For Worse* (T. Fisher Unwin, London, 1887). Jessopp was Rector of Scarning in Norfolk. *The Trials of a Country Parson* (1890) is a companion volume to this.

47. Reports of Special Assistant Poor Law Commissioners on the Employment of Women and Children in Agriculture (Parliamentary Papers, 1843, vol. XII). Wincheap is in Kent. 'Cant' = a division of land.

48. SOMERVILLE, *The Whistler at the Plough* (see note 15). The location is Sussex.

49. JESSOPP, *Arcady: For Better For Worse* (see note 46). One of his parishioners speaking.

50. GEORGE BOURNE (STURT), *The Bettesworth Book* (Lamley & Co., London, 1901). 'Bettesworth' was Frederick Grover, Sturt's gardener; Sturt never told him he was recording and publishing his conversation. Sturt described him as 'a type of his class': the 'Surrey peasant'. But the books gain their special quality from Sturt's real affection and respect for his subject.

51. Reports of Special Assistant Poor Law Commissioners on Agriculture (see note 47). 'Bridewell' = prison.

52. A. J. MUNBY, *Dorothy: A Country Story* (C. Kegan Paul, London, 1880).

53. Royal Commission on Labour: The Agricultural Labourer (Parliamentary Papers, 1893–4, vol. XXV). Mrs Black was the steward's wife at Ilderton, Northumberland.

54. THOMAS MILLER, *Pictures of Country Life* (David Bogue, London, 1847). Miller is a neglected writer, whose rural books contain many beautiful passages, though he was unfortunately forced to re-use and re-work his best material too often for comfort. Statute or 'Mop' fairs were hiring fairs, at which farmers and labourers mutually bound themselves to a year's employment and service. The 'fastenpenny' sealed the deal, like the King's shilling for those joining the army. Other nineteenth-century writers condemned the fairs as rowdy and outdated, offering opportunities for vice and depravity, and they gradually died out. It was not unusual for labourers to change employment each year. Hardy describes the Dorchester Statute fair in *Far From the Madding Crowd*, Chapter 6. John Clare noted in his journal for Tuesday 21 September 1824, 'The Statute & a very wet day for it the lasses do not lift up their gowns to show taper ancles & white stockings but on the contrary to hide dirty ones.'

55. FRED KITCHEN, *Brother to the Ox* (Dent, London, 1940). Kitchen wrote this autobiography with the encouragement of a WEA writing class. His other books include a novel, *The Commoners* (1950), and *Life on the Land* (1941).

56. From a broadside published by H. Such, in the Bodleian Library, Firth c19 (153). I have amended 'and' to 'it' in verse 3, line 2, in the interests of clarity. Other versions replace the pointed irony of this text's penultimate verse with straightforward complaint, graphically lamenting that 'treacle, salts and jelly, you have for to drink, / For to loose you in the body and make you f—t and stink.'

57. CLARE, *Selected Poems and Prose* (see note 9).

58. JAMES REEVES, *The Idiom of the People* (Heinemann, London, 1958). One of a number of poignant crow-scaring chants. Collected by Cecil Sharp from John Durbin at Harptree, 1904.

59. ARCH, *Life* (see note 41).

60. Reports of Special Assistant Poor Law Commissioners on Agriculture (see note 47). Godolphin Osborne was Rector of Bryanston-cum-Durweston, Dorsetshire.

61. ASHBY, *Joseph Ashby of Tysoe* (see note 16).

62. REG GROVES, *Sharpen the Sickle: The History of the Farm Workers' Union* (Porcupine Press, London, 1949). Groves notes that 'this song, a traditional and local one, was much sung in the Wilford Hundred of Suffolk during the strikes and lock-outs of 1873 and 1874.'

63. ARTHUR RANDELL, *Fenland Memories*, ed. Enid Porter (Routledge & Kegan Paul, London, 1969). Mr Randell was born in 1901.

64. THOMAS, *Collected Poems* (see note 2).

65. CLIFFORD MORSLEY (ed.), *News from the English Countryside 1750–1850* (Harrap, London, 1979). Reprinted from the *Stamford News* in the *Leicester Chronicle*, 3 February 1827.

66. ELIZA GUTCH, *County Folklore VI: East Riding of Yorkshire* (The Folklore Society, London, 1912).

67. ARCH, *Life* (see note 41).

68. From a broadside published by H. F. Sefton of Worcester, in the Bodleian Library, Firth b34 (229).

69. GARTH CHRISTIAN (ed.), *A Victorian Poacher: James Hawker's Journal* (Oxford University Press, London, 1961). From the introduction.

70. ARCH, *Life* (see note 41). The Act in question is the Poaching Prevention Act of 1862.

71. CHARLES KINGSLEY, *The Poems of Charles Kingsley* (Oxford University Press, London, 1913). This poem is also known as 'A Rough Rhyme on a Rough Matter'. Kingsley included it in *Yeast* (1851) as the work of the novel's hero Lancelot Smith.

72. CHRISTIAN (ed.), *A Victorian Poacher* (see note 69). A comparable and equally good account of poaching from the inside is *I Walked By Night* by 'The King of the Norfolk Poachers', ed. Lilias Rider Haggard (1935).

73. RICHARD HEATH, *The English Peasant* (T. Fisher Unwin, London, 1893). This little exchange is reported from a Kent night-school.

74. WILLIAM COBBETT, *Rural Rides* (Dent, London, 1912; Penguin, Harmondsworth, 1967; first published 1821–32). Dated 31 August 1823, Kent.

75. ASHBY, *Joseph Ashby of Tysoe* (see note 16).

76. JOHN HARRIS, *My Autobiography* (Hamilton Adams & Co., London, 1882). Harris was a Cornish tin-miner poet. He looked back on the agricultural work of his childhood with some nostalgia.

77. THOMAS HARDY, *Collected Poems* (Macmillan, London, 1976).

78. ALFRED WILLIAMS, *A Wiltshire Village* (Duckworth, London, 1912). The village is South Marston. It is possible that the old man was worried about having acquired secret horsemen's knowledge, accompanied by semi-magical rituals. Williams tells us that 'he was generally off on the road somewhere with his team of horses'. George Ewart Evans has explored this area of traditional belief in a number of books, notably *Horse Power and Magic* (1979).

79. GEORGE BOURNE (STURT), *Memoirs of a Surrey Labourer* (Duckworth, London, 1907). It is Bettesworth talking.

80. BOURNE, *The Bettesworth Book* (see note 50).

81. HARDY, *Collected Poems* (see note 77).

82. RANDELL, *Fenland Memories* (see note 63).

83. COBBETT, *Rural Rides* (see note 74). Dated 31 August 1823, Kent.

84. ASHBY, *Joseph Ashby of Tysoe* (see note 16). Joseph Ashby describes Arch's Tysoe meeting in an article entitled 'Union Meeting' in *Land Magazine* (July 1899), under the pen-name J. A. Benson.

85. CLARE, *Selected Poems and Prose* (see note 9).

86. MORSLEY, *News From the English Countryside* (see note 65). From the *News of the World*, 24 March 1844. Threats and arson such as this reached their peak in 1830, but lingered on, as this report shows. For further information about rural unrest at this period *see* E. Hobsbawm and G. Rudé, *Captain Swing* (1969) and J. P. D. Dunbabin (ed.), *Rural Discontent in Nineteenth Century Britain* (1974).

87. WILLIAMS, *A Wiltshire Village* (see note 78).

88. From a broadside published by Henson of Northampton, in the Bodleian Library, Firth c16 (300).

89. L. MARION SPRINGALL, *Labouring Life in Norfolk Villages 1834–1914* (George Allen & Unwin, London, 1936). From a letter to the *Eastern Weekly Press* (1874) by Sands, a Docking agricultural labourer.

90. ARCH, *Life* (see note 41).

91. C. HENRY WARREN, *Happy Countryman* (Geoffrey Bles, London and Aylesbury, 1939). The life of Mark Thurston of Essex.

92. CHRISTOPHER HOLDENBY, *The Folk of the Furrow* (Smith, Elder & Co., London, 1913). Holdenby made an honourable attempt to share the lives of agricultural workers before writing about them; the prevalence of 'sir' in the comments addressed to him shows he did not entirely succeed.

93. ARCH, *Life* (see note 41).

94. RICHARD HEATH, *The English Peasant* (see note 73). The scene is a 'poor wretched' cottage in a village two miles from Alcester in South Warwickshire.

95. ARCH, *Life* (see note 41).

96. THOMAS HARDY, 'The Dorsetshire Labourer' (*Longman's Magazine*, July 1883; reprinted in H. Orel (ed.), *Thomas Hardy's Personal Writings* (1967)). The old man is listening to Arch speak.

97. ARCH, *Life* (see note 41). A song popular at union meetings.

98. SPRINGALL, *Labouring Life in Norfolk Villages* (see note 89). A Wymondham labourer, 1872.

99. ROWNTREE and KENDALL, *How the Labourer Lives* (see note 12). Mr Finch lived in Berkshire.

100. ARCH, *Life* (see note 41).

101. ARCH, *Life* (see note 41).

102. W. H. HUDSON, *A Shepherd's Life* (Methuen, London, 1910). This conversation took place in a churchyard in Wiltshire.

103. ASHBY, *Joseph Ashby of Tysoe* (see note 16).

104. MAUD KARPELES, *Cecil Sharp's Collection of English Folk Songs* (Oxford University Press, London, 1974). Sung by Shepherd Haden (83) at Bampton, Oxfordshire, 6 September 1909.

105. THOMAS HARDY, *Far From the Madding Crowd* (Macmillan, London, 1974; Penguin, Harmondsworth, 1978; first published 1874).

106. CLARE, *The Shepherd's Calendar*, 'June' (see note 4).

107. BOB COPPER, *A Song for Every Season* (Heinemann, London, 1971). The Copper family come from Rottingdean in Sussex; their singing tradition can be heard on a four-record set, also called *A Song for Every Season* (Leader, LEA 4046–9, 1971).

108. COPPER, *A Song for Every Season* (see previous note).

109. CLARE, *The Shepherd's Calendar*, 'June' (see note 4).

110. FRANK PURSLOW, *Marrow Bones* (English Folk Dance and Song Society, London, 1965). Collected by H. E. D. Hammond from William Miller, Wotton Fitzpaine, Dorset, April 1906.

111. VITA SACKVILLE-WEST, *The Land* (William Heinemann, London, 1926).

112. FRANCIS KILVERT, *Diary*, ed. W. Plomer (Cape, London, 1938–40). Entry for 22 July 1873.

113. KITCHEN, *Brother to the Ox* (see note 55).

114. ASHBY, *Joseph Ashby of Tysoe* (see note 16).

115. S. O. ADDY, *Household Tales with other Traditional Remains* (Nutt, London and Pawson & Brailsford, Sheffield, 1895). One of a series of numskull tales about the village of Austwick in the West Riding.

116. THOMPSON, *Lark Rise to Candleford* (see note 7).

117. ASHBY, *Joseph Ashby of Tysoe* (see note 16).

118. W. H. HUDSON, *Afoot in England* (Hutchinson, London, 1909). This encounter took place 'near Southampton Water'.

119. HARDY, *Tess of the D'Urbervilles* (see note 29).

120. ALISON UTTLEY, *The Country Child* (Faber & Faber, London, 1931).

121. NORTHALL, *English Folk-Rhymes* (see note 20).

122. WILLIAM HENDERSON, *Notes on the Folklore of the Northern Counties of England and the Borders* (Longmans, Green & Co., London, 1866).

123. HARDY, *Collected Poems* (see note 77).

124. CLARE, *Selected Poems and Prose* (see note 9).

125. ADDY, *Household Tales* (see note 115).

126. MARSHALL, *Fenland Chronicle* (see note 42).

127. UTTLEY, *The Country Child* (see note 120).

128. PURSLOW, *Marrow Bones* (see note 110). Collected by H. E. D. Hammond from Robert Barratt, Piddletown, Dorset, October 1905. There are verbal discrepancies between this text and the version in the *Journal of the Folk-Song Society* 11, pp. 110–11. Purslow printed from Hammond's manuscripts, but the first printing does have some attractive features, notably the third verse with its 'so black as sloes', 'so white as snow' and 'In spite of all my parents'.

129. HARDY, *Collected Poems* (see note 77).

130. HOLDENBY, *The Folk of the Furrow* (see note 92).

131. RICHARD HEATH, *The English Peasant* (see note 73).

132. BOURNE, *The Bettesworth Book* (see note 50).

133. WILLIAMS, *Folk-Songs of the Upper Thames* (see note 28). Collected from Thomas Dunn, Stratton St Margaret.

134. W. J. BOWD, 'The Life of a Farmworker' in *The Countryman* LI, no. 2 (Summer 1955). Written by James Bowd in 1889, when he was sixty-six.

135. BOURNE, *Change in the Village* (see note 10).

136. HOLDENBY, *The Folk of the Furrow* (see note 92).

137. MARSHALL, *Fenland Chronicle* (see note 42). 'Gault' is a type of clay.

138. THOMPSON, *Lark Rise to Candleford* (see note 7).

139. GEORGE EWART EVANS, *The Days That We Have Seen* (Faber & Faber, London, 1975). Arthur Welton, who is speaking, was born in 1884.

140. WILLIAMS, *A Wiltshire Village* (see note 78).

141. HENDERSON, *Notes on the Folklore of the Northern Counties* (see note 122).

142. PALMER, *English Country Songs* (see note 21). From S. Baring Gould, *English Minstrelsie* (1895–7). 'Brink' = stook; 'humming' = strong; 'arrish' = stubble. Roy Palmer suggests that the final 'hallo' refers to the custom of crying largesse, by which reapers obtained cash from passers-by to fund their post-harvest celebration.

143. GEORGE EWART EVANS, *Ask the Fellows Who Cut the Hay* (Faber & Faber, London, 1956).

144. THOMPSON, *Lark Rise to Candleford* (see note 7).

145. EDWARD THOMAS, *The South Country* (Dent, London, 1909).

146. BARRETT and GARROD, *East Anglian Folklore* (see note 30).

147. RICHARD JEFFERIES, *Nature Diaries and Note-Books*, ed. S. J. Looker (Grey Walls Press, London, 1948). Entry for 16 July 1884.

148. CLARE, *The Shepherd's Calendar*, 'August' (see note 4).

149. THOMPSON, *Lark Rise to Candleford* (see note 7).

150. EDMUND BLUNDEN, *The Poems of Edmund Blunden* (Cobden-Sanderson, London, 1930).

151. Reports of the Special Assistant Poor Law Commissioners on Agriculture (see note 47).

152. GEORGE EDWARDS, *From Crow-Scaring to Westminster* (Labour Publishing Co. London, 1922). Edwards inherited Arch's mantle, founding the National Union of Agricultural Workers. His title echoes, too, Cobbett's chosen title for his unwritten memoirs, which W. Reitzel used in assembling his autobiographical writings in 1933, *The Progress of a Ploughboy to a Seat in Parliament*.

153. HARDY, *Tess of the D'Urbervilles* (see note 29).

154. MUNBY, *Dorothy* (see note 52).

155. H. RIDER HAGGARD, *A Farmer's Year* (Longman & Co., London, 1899). Haggard's survey of English agriculture, *Rural England* (1902), is an important document. Unfortunately for this anthology, he consulted exclusively with farmers, not labourers.

156. JEFFERIES, *Nature Diaries* (see note 147). Entry dated 5 August 1884.

157. PALMER, *English Country Songs* (see note 21). From H. Sumner, *The Besom Maker* (1888).

158. WARREN, *Happy Countryman* (see note 91).

159. ADDY, *Household Tales* (see note 115). Similar customs and rhymes obtained all over the country.

160. COPPER, *A Song for Every Season* (see note 107).

161. RANDELL, *Fenland Memories* (see note 63). This custom was slowly dying out during the period covered here; instead of giving a harvest supper, farmers began to give each worker a cash supplement. The custom survived longer in East Anglia, where the festival was known as 'horkey', than it did elsewhere. Often vicars sought to substitute a sedate Harvest Festival for the raucous Harvest Home.

162. REEVES, *The Idiom of the People* (see note 58). Collected by Cecil Sharp from William Shepherd (93) at Winchcomb Workhouse, 1909. According to Shepherd, this was often recited at Harvest Home. 'Boom' represents a bell. Reeves also gives a version noted in the late seventeenth century by a Dane travelling in England. The lines up to 'When did er die?' are spoken dialogue; the rest is sung. See the *Journal of the Folk-Song Society* 3, pp. 68–70, for two other versions, and 5, pp. 275–6, for a note.

163. ALFRED WILLIAMS, *Round About the Upper Thames* (Duckworth, London, 1922).

164. JOHN CLARE, 'Autobiography' in *The Prose of John Clare*, ed. J. W. and A. Tibble (Routledge & Kegan Paul, London, 1951). 'Quick-lines' are young hawthorns.

165. JOHN CLARE, *The Midsummer Cushion*, ed. A. Tibble and R. K. R. Thornton (MidNAG/Carcanet, Ashington & Manchester, 1979).

166. F. G. HEATH, *The English Peasantry* (Frederick Warne, London, 1874). Heath also wrote *The 'Romance' of Peasant Life* (1872) and *British Rural Life and Labour* (1911).

167. WILLIAMS, *A Wiltshire Village* (see note 78).

168. HARDY, *Collected Poems* (see note 77).

169. MORSLEY, *News from the English Countryside* (see note 65). From *The Falmouth Packet*, 14 November 1829. This rhyme, in many variations, was recited to apple-trees on the eve of Epiphany; sometimes cider was poured on to the earth; sometimes shots were fired near or at the tree.

170. WILLIAMS, *Round About the Upper Thames* (see note 163).

171. S. BARING GOULD, *Old Country Life* (Methuen, London, 1890). James Parsons came from Lew Down in Devon.

172. THOMPSON, *Lark Rise to Candleford* (see note 7).

173. HARDY, *Collected Poems* (see note 77).

174. PALMER, *English Country Songs* (see note 21). Collected by Cecil Sharp from Charles Parsons, Knole Farm, Long Sutton, September 1903.

175. COBBETT, *Rural Rides* (see note 74). Dated 6 August 1823, Hampshire.

176. A. J. MUNBY diary entry dated 28 January 1859, quoted in Derek Hudson, *Munby: Man of Two Worlds* (John Murray, London, 1972). Munby was obsessed by labouring women, and left an unparalleled record in still largely unpublished manuscript diaries of his encounters and conversations with all sorts of Victorian female workers. His poems, including *Dorothy*, constantly revisit the theme of romance or marriage between a high-born man and low-born woman; Munby was actually secretly married to a maid-of-all-work, Hannah Cullwick. His collection of photographs forms the basis of Michael Hiley's *Victorian Working Women: Portraits from Life* (1979).

177. MUNBY, *Dorothy* (see note 52).

178. THOMPSON, *Lark Rise to Candleford* (see note 7).

179. A. J. MUNBY diary entry dated 21 May 1864, quoted in Jennie Kitteringham, *Country Girls in 19th Century England* (History Workshop Pamphlets no. 11, 1973).

180. ARCH, *Life* (see note 41).

181. HARDY, *Collected Poems* (see note 77).

182. HARDY, *Tess of the D'Urbervilles* (see note 29).

183. EVANS, *Ask the Fellows Who Cut the Hay* (see note 143).

184. CLARE, *The Shepherd's Calendar*, 'November' (see note 4).

185. UTTLEY, *The Country Child* (see note 120).

186. CLARE, *Selected Poems and Prose* (see note 9). 'Progs' = prods. 'Croodling' and 'hirkles' both describe the act of shrinking or contracting the body from the cold.

187. CLARE, *The Prose of John Clare*, 'Autobiography' (see note 164).

188. THOMPSON, *Lark Rise to Candleford* (see note 7).

189. ADDY, *Household Tales* (see note 115).

190. KITCHEN, *Brother to the Ox* (see note 55).

191. GROVES, *Sharpen the Sickle* (see note 62). He notes this as 'a street ballad, about 1840'. The 'Whig Bastile' is the workhouse.

192. HAGGARD, *A Farmer's Year* (see note 155).

193. HAGGARD, *A Farmer's Year* (see note 155).

194. WILLIAMS, *A Wiltshire Village* (see note 78). This is Mark Titcombe, the man who believed he had sold his soul to the devil (no. 78).

195. RICHARD JEFFERIES, *Hodge and his Masters* (Smith, Elder & Co., London, 1880). Perhaps Jefferies' major work in this vein, reissued with an introduction by Andrew Rossabi (1979). This extract comes from the downbeat conclusion, 'Hodge's Last Masters'.

196. HARDY, *Collected Poems* (see note 77).

197. WILLIAMS, *A Wiltshire Village* (see note 78).

198. BOB COPPER, *Songs and Southern Breezes* (Heinemann, London, 1973). This unattributed poem comes from the notebooks of Frank 'Mush' Bond of Dummer.

199. WILLIAMS, *Folk-Songs of the Upper Thames* (see note 28). Collected from Mrs Hedges, Purton, Wilts.

200. CLARE, *The Shepherd's Calendar*, 'December' (see note 4).

201. THOMAS HARDY, *The Return of the Native* (Penguin, Harmondsworth, 1978; first published 1878).

202. WILLIAMS, *Folk-Songs of the Upper Thames* (see note 28). Collected from 'Wassail' Harvey of Cricklade and E. Smart of Oaksey, Wilts. A characteristically inventive verbal distortion in some texts of this song is the substitution of the phrase 'We'll sail' for the archaic 'Wassail'.

203. RUTH L. TONGUE, *Forgotten Folk Tales of the English Counties* (Routledge & Kegan Paul, London, 1970). A luminous nativity story 'Told to her family by a Wincanton farmer's wife, about 1900', and retold with Ruth Tongue's characteristic vigorous delicacy. A 'nirrip' is a young jenny-ass.

204. KILVERT, *Diary* (see note 112). Entry dated 4 January 1878.

205. HARDY, *Collected Poems* (see note 77).

206. CHARLOTTE MEW, *Collected Poems and Prose* (Carcanet, Manchester, and Virago, London, 1982).

207. THOMAS, *Collected Poems* (see note 2).

208. RUTH L. TONGUE, *The Chime Child* (Routledge & Kegan Paul, London, 1968).

209. HARDY, *Collected Poems* (see note 77).

FURTHER READING

J. L. and Barbara Hammond, *The Village Labourer*, new edition ed. G. E. Mingay (Longman, London, 1978)

Pamela Horn, *Labouring Life in the Victorian Countryside* (Gill & Macmillan, Dublin, 1976)

Pamela Horn, *The Victorian Country Child* (The Roundwood Press, Kineton, 1974)

W. J. Keith, *The Rural Tradition* (Harvester Press, Hassocks, 1975)

G. E. Mingay, *Rural Life in Victorian England* (Heinemann, London, 1977)

G. E. Mingay (ed.), *The Victorian Countryside*, 2 vols. (Routledge & Kegan Paul, London, 1981)

Raphael Samuel (ed.), *Village Life and Labour* (Routledge & Kegan Paul, London, 1975)

Rayner Unwin, *The Rural Muse* (George Allen & Unwin, London, 1954)

Merryn Williams, *Thomas Hardy and Rural England* (Macmillan, London, 1972)

Raymond Williams, *The Country and the City* (Chatto & Windus, London, 1973)

INDEX OF SOURCES

(Numbers quoted are extract numbers)

ACKNOWLEDGEMENTS

We are indebted to the copyright holders for permission to reprint certain passages:

M. K. Ashby: extracts from *Joseph Ashby of Tysoe 1859–1919* reprinted by permission of the author and Cambridge University Press;

W. H. Barrett & R. P. Garrod: extracts from *East Anglian Folklore and Other Tales* reprinted by permission of Routledge & Kegan Paul PLC;

E. Blunden: 'Gleaning' from *The Poems of Edmund Blunden* reprinted by permission of A. D. Peters & Co. Ltd;

W. J. Bowd: extract from 'The Life of a Farmworker' reprinted by permission of *The Countryman*, Burford, Oxfordshire;

J. Clare: lines from *The Shepherd's Calendar*, edited by Eric Robinson and Geoffrey Summerfield, copyright © Oxford University Press, 1964, reprinted by permission of Oxford University Press; extracts from *Selected Poems and Prose of John Clare*, edited by Eric Robinson and Geoffrey Summerfield, copyright © Eric Robinson, 1967, reproduced by permission of Curtis Brown Ltd;

B. Copper: extracts from *A Song for Every Season* reprinted by permission of William Heinemann Ltd;

G. E. Evans: extracts from *The Days That We Have Seen* and *Ask the Fellows Who Cut the Hay* reprinted by permission of Faber and Faber Ltd;

R. Groves: 'The Crow Boy' and 'The Honest Ploughman' from *Sharpen the Sickle!* reprinted by permission of the author;

E. Gutch: 'The Sledmere Poachers' from *County Folklore VI* reprinted by permission of the Folklore Society;

F. Hamer: 'Ox Plough Song' and 'Pace Egg Song – Chipping' from *Garners Gay* copyright © Chappell Music Ltd, 1967, reprinted by kind permission of Chappell Music Ltd;

J. Hawker: extracts from *James Hawker's Journal: A Victorian Poacher*, edited by Garth Christian, copyright © Oxford University Press, 1961, reprinted by permission of Oxford University Press;

R. Jefferies: extracts from Richard Jefferies, *Nature Diaries and Note-Books*, edited by S. J. Looker, reprinted by permission of Mrs M. H. Jacques;

F. Kilvert: extracts from *Kilvert's Diary*, edited by William Plomer, reprinted by permission of Mrs Sheila Hooper and Jonathan Cape Ltd;

R. Kipling: 'A Charm' from *Rewards and Fairies* reprinted by permission of The National Trust, Macmillan, London, Ltd, and Doubleday and Company, Inc.;

F. Kitchen: extracts from *Brother to the Ox* reprinted by permission of J. M. Dent and Sons Ltd;

I. Mead: extract from *The Life Story of an Essex Lad* reprinted by permission of A. Driver and Sons Ltd;

S. Marshall: extracts from *Fenland Chronicle* reprinted by permission of the author and Cambridge University Press;

J. Masefield: extracts from 'The Everlasting Mercy' reprinted by permission of the Society of Authors as the literary representative of the Estate of John Masefield, and reprinted with permission of Macmillan Publishing Company from *Collected Poems* by John Masefield. Copyright 1912 by Macmillan Publishing Co., Inc., renewed 1940 by John Masefield;

C. Mew: 'Old Shepherd's Prayer' from Charlotte Mew, *Collected Poems and Prose*, edited by Val Warner, reprinted by permission of Carcanet Press and Virago;

A. J. Munby: extracts from his diaries reprinted by permission of the Master and Fellows of Trinity College, Cambridge;

F. Purslow: 'The Bonny Labouring Boy' and 'Sheep-shearing Song' from *Marrow Bones* copyright © Chappell Music Ltd, 1965, and 'When this old hat was new' from *Foggy Dew* copyright © Chappell Music Ltd, 1974, reprinted by kind permission of Chappell Music Ltd;

A. Randell: extracts from *Fenland Memories* reprinted by permission of Routledge & Kegan Paul PLC;

C. Morsley: extracts from *News from the English Countryside 1750–1850* reprinted by permission of Harrap Ltd;

B. S. Rowntree & M. Kendall: extracts from *How the Labourer Lives* reprinted by permission of the Joseph Rowntree Charitable Trust;

V. Sackville-West: extract from *The Land* copyright © Nigel Nicolson, reprinted by permission of Nigel Nicolson, executor to the late V. Sackville-West;

C. Sharp: 'A Harvest Song' from J. Reeves, *The Idiom of the People* reprinted by permission of Bird & Bird for the estate of Cecil Sharp; 'Once I was a shepherd boy' from Maud Karpeles, *Cecil Sharp's Collection of English Folk Songs* (1974) by permission of Oxford University Press;

F. Thompson: extracts from *Lark Rise to Candleford* (1945) reprinted by permission of Oxford University Press;

R. L. Tongue: extracts from *The Chime Child* and *Forgotten Folk Tales of the English Counties* reprinted by permission of Routledge & Kegan Paul PLC;

A. Uttley: extracts from *The Country Child* reprinted by permission of Faber and
  Faber Ltd;

D. Wordsworth: extract from *Journals of Dorothy Wordsworth*, edited by E. de
  Selincourt, reprinted by permission of Macmillan, London and Basingstoke,
  Ltd

Every effort has been made to trace copyright holders. The publishers would be
interested to hear from any copyright holders not here acknowledged.

MORE ABOUT PENGUINS, PELICANS
AND PUFFINS

For further information about books available from Penguins please write to Dept EP, Penguin Books Ltd, Harmondsworth, Middlesex UB7 0DA.

In the U.S.A.: For a complete list of books available from Penguins in the United States write to Dept DG, Penguin Books, 299 Murray Hill Parkway, East Rutherford, New Jersey 07073.

In Canada: For a complete list of books available from Penguins in Canada write to Penguin Books Canada Ltd, 2801 John Street, Markham, Ontario L3R 1B4.

In Australia: For a complete list of books available from Penguins in Australia write to the Marketing Department, Penguin Books Australia Ltd, P.O. Box 257, Ringwood, Victoria 3134.

In New Zealand: For a complete list of books available from Penguins in New Zealand write to the Marketing Department, Penguin Books (N.Z.) Ltd, P.O. Box 4019, Auckland 10.

In India: For a complete list of books available from Penguins in India write to Penguin Overseas Ltd, 706 Eros Apartments, 56 Nehru Place, New Delhi 110019.

A RADICAL READER

The struggle for change in England, 1381–1914

Edited by Christopher Hampton

This major new anthology spans five hundred years of radical protest from the Peasants' Revolt to the First World War.

In the richness and variety of its documentation, it provides an alternative political and social history of England; a history which puts at its centre the actions of ordinary men and women discovering the issues that govern their lives and the common interests vital to them. This is history as creative defiance, as communal action, involving the intellectual and imaginative witness of those among the privileged – poets, writers and thinkers – who have had the strength and courage to make themselves passionate spokesmen for the dispossessed.

Here are passages from Froissart's *Chronicles*, More's *Utopia*, Hobbes's *Leviathan*, Bunyan's *Pilgrim's Progress*, and Mary Wollstonecraft's *A Vindication of the Rights of Woman*. Here too are extracts from the writings of Wycliff, Wyatt, Skelton, Shakespeare, Bacon, Milton, Winstanley, Marvell, Swift, Blake, Wordsworth, Cobbett, Byron, Shelley, Dickens and Marx – plus a wealth of hitherto inaccessible documents, tracts, songs, pamphlets and newspaper articles that challenge the injustices of the status quo and together bear witness to a vital and unbroken line of radical protest.

A Radical Reader is arranged chronologically, and includes a full introduction with linked commentary and a bibliography by the editor, Christopher Hampton.

The Penguin English Library

LANDSCAPE WITH FIGURES
An Anthology of Richard Jefferies's Prose
Chosen and introduced by Richard Mabey

Richard Jefferies (1848–87) was probably the most imaginative and certainly the least conventional of country writers. He did not work the land, nor did he always live in the country, and yet in his articles and essays almost all our current ideas about rural life can be found.

He was passionate, inconsistent and insatiably curious about the countryside. Who does it belong to? Is it a place, an experience or a way of life? Ranging over these questions his prolific output included the letters to *The Times* that began his career, technical pieces for the farming press, propaganda for Tory journals, mystical works and meditations; while he is best known as the pioneer of the 'country diary', vivid and idiosyncratic ramblings on orchards, ants, stiles, the ague, the weather and 'noises in the air'.

As this superbly edited volume illustrates, Jefferies's writings form one of the finest reflections of the ambivalences and paradoxes that emerge when people live close to nature.

The Penguin English Library

EDWARD THOMAS
Selected Poems and Prose

Edited by David Wright

The prose of Edward Thomas was voluminous and various: between 1897 and 1917 he published nearly thirty volumes of topography, biography and literary criticism. These books were often about the country writers such as Richard Jefferies or George Borrow whom Thomas most admired, and required him to travel the length of the country gathering material. Yet he regarded them as literary drudgery, a necessary means of supporting his family. Retrospectively, they have been seen as a lifetime's preparation for two years of inspired poetry.

In 1914 Thomas began to write verse, and by 1917, when he was killed at Passchendaele, he had earned his place as the last of the English poets who (beginning with Wordsworth) recorded and elegized the slow destruction of the rural England and its culture that they so cherished.

Penguin Poetry

THE PENGUIN BOOK OF EVERYDAY VERSE
Social and Documentary Poetry 1250–1916
Edited by David Wright

'The best anthology of the year' – Martin Seymour-Smith in the *Financial Times*

The Penguin Book of Everyday Verse presents poems, gathered from a whole variety of sources, that illuminate, describe or otherwise record daily life in Britain – in all a rich, exciting and unique anthology.

'Verses about work and weddings and hangings and clothes and food and drink and festivals and fashions of all kinds . . . David Wright has compiled an extraordinary anthology' – Robert Nye in *The Times*

'The selection runs from Edward Thomas and Hardy through Locker-Lampson (a brilliant and neglected writer), Byron, Wordsworth, Stephen Duck, Swift and Jonson back to Chaucer . . . The most immediately entertaining and enjoyable verse anthology that I have encountered: which by now is saying a lot' – John Holloway in *The Times Higher Education Supplement*

Between Earth and Sky chronicles the death-throes of a tradition of life lived close to the land and the seasons.

It was a harsh existence and this evocative anthology of prose and verse makes no attempt to sentimentalize the past. As the compiler notes in his Introduction: 'We should not idealize the workfolk in these pages or their way of life. But if we cannot wholeheartedly envy them, we can celebrate them. We certainly cannot look down on them, seeing how much they made of their little, and how little we make of our much.'

Included in it are the writings of John Clare, William Cobbett, George Bourne, Flora Thompson and Francis Kilvert, as well as many lesser-known voices from diaries, songs, personal accounts and the reports of various Poor Law Commissions. In all, a matchless glimpse into a pattern of living which vanished during the Great War.

The cover shows a detail from "Binding Sheaves" by Sir George Clausen
(photo: Christie, Manson and Woods)

Cover design by John Gorham

U.K.   £2.95
AUST. $7.95
(recommended)
N.Z. $10.95
CAN. $7.95

Poetr
Literatur
ISBN 0 1
059.005